Nick Vandome

P9-CSE-196

Kindle Fire
HDX

in
easy steps

Also covers Kindle Fire

In easy steps is an imprint of In Easy Steps Limited
16 Hamilton Terrace · Holly Walk · Leamington Spa
Warwickshire · United Kingdom · CV32 4LY
www.ineasysteps.com

Copyright © 2014 by In Easy Steps Limited. All rights reserved. No part
of this book may be reproduced or transmitted in any form or by any
means, electronic or mechanical, including photocopying, recording,
or by any information storage or retrieval system, without prior
written permission from the publisher.

Notice of Liability

Every effort has been made to ensure that this book contains accurate
and current information. However, In Easy Steps Limited and the
author shall not be liable for any loss or damage suffered by readers
as a result of any information contained herein.

Trademarks

Kindle, Kindle Fire and Amazon are trademarks of Amazon.com, Inc.
or its affiliates. All other trademarks are acknowledged as belonging
to their respective companies.

In Easy Steps Limited supports The Forest Stewardship Council (FSC),
the leading international forest certification organisation. All our titles
that are printed on Greenpeace approved FSC certified paper carry the
FSC logo.

MIX
Paper from
responsible sources
FSC® C020837

Printed and bound in the United Kingdom

ISBN 978-1-84078-624-8

Contents

1 First Fire Steps

The tablet computer market is becoming increasingly competitive and the Kindle Fire is fast establishing itself as a significant player in this arena. This chapter introduces the Kindle Fire and shows how to set it up and use the online Amazon Cloud Drive too.

About the Kindle Fire

Mobility is now a key word in the world of computing and tablet computers are beginning to play a significant role in how we all communicate and access information. The Kindle Fire is a fully-fledged tablet that has evolved out of the Kindle eReader that was originally designed for reading books, newspapers and magazines. The Kindle Fire HD and HDX take this several steps further, with functionality to:

- Surf the web and access your favorite social networking sites
- Use email
- Listen to music
- Download apps
- Play games
- Watch movies and TV shows
- Read all of your favorite books

The Kindle Fire HDX has a superior quality screen over the HD version and a few additional features, such as the Mayday help service, but in most respects the functionality of the two models is the same.

The New icon pictured above indicates a new or enhanced feature introduced with the latest version of the Kindle Fire HDX.

...cont'd

Kindle Fire and Amazon

One of the first things to say about the Kindle Fire is that it is an Amazon product and most things on it are linked to Amazon in one way or another. To use the Kindle Fire you need to have an Amazon Account with a username and password. If you do not already have one this will be set up if you buy your Kindle Fire from the Amazon website or, if you buy it from another retailer, you can create an Amazon Account during the setup process. Most of the content in terms of books, movies, music and apps comes from the Amazon online store, although there are some items that you can also upload to your Kindle Fire.

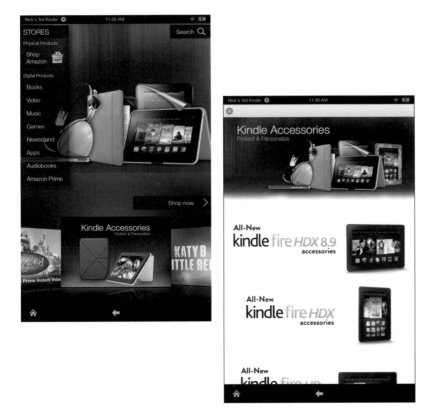

Beware

Although it is possible to use other apps on the Kindle Fire, such as Android ones, this is not recommended as it can involve processes that could harm your Kindle Fire. It is best to stick to the items available through the Amazon Shop and Appstore.

The Kindle Fire HD has a standard model and an HDX model: both have 7-inch screen and 8.9-inch models. The Kindle Fire HD has 8, 16 or 32GB of storage and the HDX comes with 16, 32 or 64GB of storage, so the whole range is powerful enough to be able to store the content you need, whether at home or on the move when traveling.

Don't forget

A case can be bought for the Kindle Fire HD and HDX, to protect the screen and also, in some instances, act as a stand.

Specifications

The specifications for the Kindle Fire HD and HDX are:

Kindle Fire HD 7-inch

- 7-inch (diagonally) 1280 x 800 pixel HD display

- Dolby audio and dual-driver stereo speakers

- Dual band Wi-Fi for fast downloads and HD streaming

- 1.5 GHz dual-core processor

- 8 or 16GB storage, plus free unlimited cloud storage for all of your Amazon content (see Chapter Four)

- Up to 10 hours battery life for mixed use including reading and surfing the web

- Kindle FreeTime for creating individual profiles for children and specifying the content they can use (see Chapter Twelve)

- Fire OS 3.0 Mojito operating system

Kindle Fire HD 8.9-inch

- 8.9-inch (diagonally) 1920 x 1200 pixel HD display

- Dolby audio and dual-driver stereo speakers

- Dual band, dual antenna Wi-Fi

- 1.5 GHz dual-core processor

- 16 or 32GB storage, plus free unlimited cloud storage for all of your Amazon content (see Chapter Four)

- An HDMI port for viewing your content on your TV or other devices

- Front-facing HD camera

- Up to 10 hours battery life for mixed use including reading and surfing the web

- Kindle FreeTime for creating individual profiles for children and specifying the content they can use (see Chapter Twelve)

- Customized operating system based on Android 4.0.3

The Kindle Fire HD 7-inch model does not have a built-in camera.

The Kindle Fire HD 8.9-inch model is the only one in the range that has an HDMI port for connecting to a High Definition Television.

Kindle Fire HDX 7-inch

- 7-inch (diagonally) 1920 x 1200 pixel HDX display

- Dolby audio and dual-driver stereo speakers and built-in microphone

- Dual band, dual antenna Wi-Fi

- 2.2 GHz dual-core processor

- 16, 32 or 64GB of storage, plus free unlimited cloud storage for all of your Amazon content (see Chapter Four)

- Front-facing HD camera

- Up to 11 hours battery life for mixed use including reading and surfing the web

- Kindle FreeTime for creating individual profiles for children and specifying the content they can use (see Chapter Twelve)

- Fire OS 3.0 Mojito operating system

Kindle Fire HDX 8.9-inch

- 8.9-inch (diagonally) 2560 x 1600 pixel HDX display

- Dolby audio and dual-driver stereo speakers and built-in microphone

- Dual band, dual antenna Wi-Fi

- 2.2 GHz dual-core processor

- 16, 32 or 64GB of storage, plus free unlimited cloud storage for all of your Amazon content (see Chapter Four)

- Front-facing HD camera and rear-facing 8MP camera

- Up to 12 hours battery life for mixed use including reading and surfing the web

- Kindle FreeTime for creating individual profiles for children and specifying the content they can use (see Chapter Twelve)

- Fire OS 3.0 Mojito operating system

The HDX models of the Kindle Fire also have a 'Mayday' button which can be used to connect to a member of Amazon support staff, via a video chat, to get online support for your Kindle (see page 47).

11

Both of the HDX models have options for including 3G/4G functionality, for connecting to the Internet on the go, with an appropriate mobile service provider, which incurs additional cost.

Fire OS 3 Mojito

All consumer computers have an operating system, whether they are desktops, laptops or tablets. For desktops and laptops the most familiar are Windows or OS X for Macs, while for tablets the main choice is between the Android operating system or iOS for Apple tablets.

The operating system for the latest models of the Kindle Fire HD 7-inch and the HDX, 7-inch and 8.9-inch, is called Fire OS 3 Mojito. This is an operating system that is unique to the Kindle Fire, although it is based on Android. It is known as a 'forked' system, which means it started as Android and was then developed along a different route, while still maintaining the foundation of the original Android operating system. This has resulted in a unique Kindle Fire user interface, coupled with online access to cloud storage via the Amazon website, where you can store content that has been bought with your Kindle Fire, or created with it.

As in common with other tablet operating systems, Fire OS 3 Mojito uses a touchscreen interface. This means that all of the operations on the tablets are conducted by tapping, swiping or pinching on the screen. For instance, to open an app you tap on it once and to move between screens, such as the Carousel Home screen, you swipe from right to left.

The Kindle Fire HD 8.9-inch model runs on the previous version of the Fire OS operating system, not Fire OS 3.0.

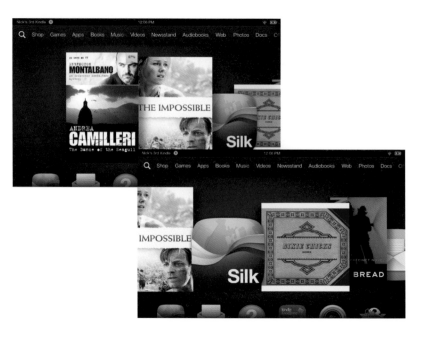

...cont'd

Checking your OS version

Most operating systems for tablets are updated to a new version on a regular basis, generally between a year and 18 months. However, in between this timescale there are often minor upgrades within the same version of the software, which become version 1.1, 1.2, etc. It is always best to update your operating system when you can, so that you are always up-to-date.

You can check the current version of your Kindle operating system, and see if there are any updates available, from within the **Settings** section. To do this:

1 Swipe down from the top of the screen and tap on the **Settings** button

2 Tap on the **Device** button

3 Tap on the **System Updates** button

4 Tap on the **Check Now** button to see if there are any updates to be installed

5 If your operating system is up-to-date it will state **No updates found**

When there are updates to the operating system you will normally be alerted to this. However, it is still a good idea to check periodically too.

13

Buttons and Ports

The buttons and ports on the Kindle Fire are located along the edges of the device and consist of:

- On/Off button. Press this once to turn on the Kindle Fire or put it into sleep mode. Press and hold to turn it off.

- Volume buttons.

- Stereo jack, for use with headphones or to connect to a stereo system.

- Micro-B Connector for charging the Kindle Fire. This connects with a USB port on a computer or the Kindle Powerfast Charger.

Press and hold the On/Off button to turn your Kindle Fire on or off. Press it once to put it to sleep mode when it is not in use. Press it again to wake the Kindle Fire up from sleep. This will activate the Lock Screen, which can be opened by swiping the padlock icon to the left.

The Micro-B Connector is inserted into the Kindle Fire and the USB connector is inserted into the USB port on the Powerfast Charger or a computer's USB port.

On/Off button

Speakers

Volume buttons

Stereo jack

Micro-B Connector (for charging or connecting to a computer)

Setting up your Kindle Fire

When you first turn on your Kindle Fire you will be taken through the setup process. This only takes a few minutes and once it has been completed you will be ready to use your Kindle Fire and all of the related Amazon services. The elements of the setup process are:

- Select a language (tap on the **Continue** button after each step).

- Select your Wi-Fi connection (this can also be done at a later time). Your home Wi-Fi should show up for selection at this point.

- Register your Kindle Fire with your Amazon Account, or create a new Amazon Account.

- Select your time zone.

- Link to your Facebook and Twitter accounts (this is optional).

Once you have completed the setup, your Kindle Fire will be ready for use; there are no other system requirements. The first thing you will see is the Kindle Fire Home screen, which is in the form of the Carousel. See pages 24-27 for more information about using this. There is also a Lock Screen that is activated when the Kindle Fire is put to sleep. This contains promotions from Amazon. This can be turned off for a fee of US $15 (UK £10) *(correct at the time of printing)*. Drag the padlock to the left to access the Carousel from the Lock Screen.

Don't forget

If you do not have an Amazon account you will be asked to create one when you first turn on your Kindle Fire. You do not have to do so at this stage, but you will need an account if you want to download anything from the Amazon Appstore.

Battery and Charging

Battery life is important for any tablet device and the Kindle Fire can be used for up to 10-11 hours from a single charge for general use such as surfing the web, composing emails, reading, listening to music and viewing videos. It comes with a Micro-B Connector that can be used to charge the Kindle Fire. There are two options for this:

- **Charging with a separate AC Adapter**. This comes in the form of the Kindle PowerFast adapter. The Micro-B Connector attaches to the adapter with a USB connector and the adapter can then be plugged into the mains power.

Hot tip

It is best to charge the battery fully each time it is connected to the charger.

- **Charging with a computer**. The Kindle Fire can also be charged by connecting the USB end of the Micro-B Connector to a Windows or Mac computer. However, this takes longer to charge than the PowerFast adapter.

The Kindle Fire charges in approximately four hours using the PowerFast adapter, but up to 13.5 hours if it is connected to a computer via a USB port.

The Kindle Fire charges more quickly if it is in sleep mode and even more quickly if it is turned off. However, it can still be used as normal while it is being charged, if required.

Don't forget

A spare PowerFast charger can be bought, in case you want to use it in more than one location.

Changing the Kindle's Name

When you initially set up your Kindle Fire it will be given a default name based on your own Amazon Account name, e.g. Nick's Kindle Fire. This is displayed in the top left-hand corner on the Status Bar at the top of the screen. However, this can be changed to anything of your own choosing. To do this:

1 Log in to your online Amazon Account

2 Under the **Your Account** heading, click on the **Manage Your Kindle** link from the available options

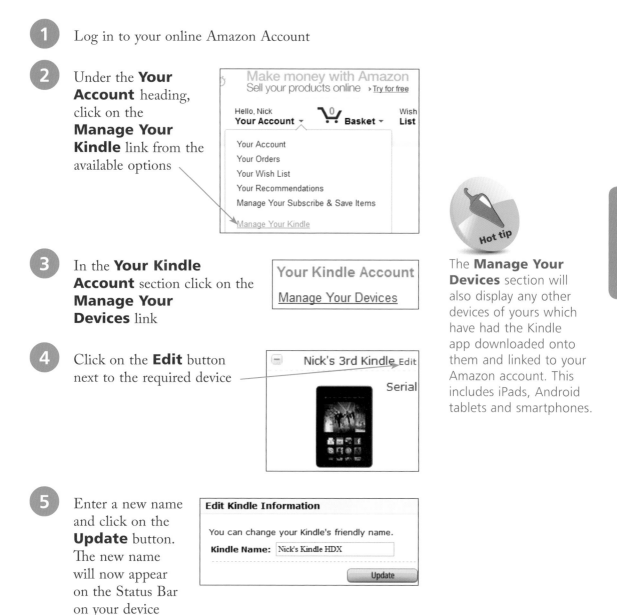

17

3 In the **Your Kindle Account** section click on the **Manage Your Devices** link

Hot tip

The **Manage Your Devices** section will also display any other devices of yours which have had the Kindle app downloaded onto them and linked to your Amazon account. This includes iPads, Android tablets and smartphones.

4 Click on the **Edit** button next to the required device

5 Enter a new name and click on the **Update** button. The new name will now appear on the Status Bar on your device

Shopping on the Kindle

The Kindle Fire is an Amazon product and it is unashamedly linked to a wide range of content from the Amazon website. This include books, games, apps and music. This can all be accessed from the Shop button on the top Navigation Bar. To do this:

Don't forget

You must have an Amazon account with a credit or debit card registered with it in order to buy items view the Amazon Shop.

1 Tap on the **Shop** button at the top of the Kindle Fire window – this can also be accessed using the Store button from individual sections

2 The main Shop window contains a rotating range of promotional items. Tap on the buttons at the bottom of the window to view specific categories

Beware

Content can be downloaded from the Amazon Shop without the need for a password (although one can be set, see page 181) so be careful if someone else is using your Kindle Fire, as it will still be linked to your account.

3 Content can be downloaded for specific categories such as Apps, Books and Games

4 Tap on items on the Home screen to view more details

Using the Amazon Cloud

Another integral part of the Kindle Fire is the Amazon Cloud. This is available on the Amazon website once you have bought a Kindle Fire and consists of:

- **The Cloud** for storing content that has been purchased from Amazon. This includes items such as eBooks and music that have been bought from Amazon. Once this is done, the content is not only available on your Kindle Fire, it is also stored, free of charge, in the Amazon Cloud. All of your compatible purchased content is stored in this way and it can then be downloaded to other Kindles, or by the Kindle app on other tablets and smartphones.

- **The Amazon Cloud Drive**. This can be used to upload your own content, including photos, music and documents, which will then be available on your Kindle Fire. You get 5GB of free storage in the Amazon Cloud Drive but you can buy additional space if required *(correct at the time of printing)*.

- **The Cloud Drive Desktop App**. This is an app that can be downloaded to make it easier to add content to your Cloud Drive. You do not have to use it, as you can upload content directly to the Cloud Drive, but it makes the process easier and can be used on Windows and Mac computers. You will be prompted to download the Desktop App when you start to upload content through the Cloud Drive.

- **The Cloud Player**. This can be used to upload your own music, which will then be available on the Kindle Fire. It can be downloaded  from the Cloud Drive and then the Amazon Music Importer can be used to scan your computer for music to upload.

For more information about using the Amazon Cloud see Chapter Four.

The Amazon Cloud stores content that can then be used on your Kindle Fire. You can also access it through the Amazon website.

Amazon Prime

When you buy a Kindle Fire you are entitled to a free month's trial of the Amazon Prime service. This consists of streaming of movies and TV shows and a virtual lending library where you can borrow one book a month, free of charge and with no due dates. You also get unlimited free two-day delivery (US, one-day in the UK) on Amazon items. To use Amazon Prime:

Amazon Prime membership costs $99/per year in the US and £79/per year in the UK *(correct at the time of printing)*.

 Tap on the **Books** link on the main Navigation Bar on the Home screen

2 Tap on the **Store** button at the top of your Books Library

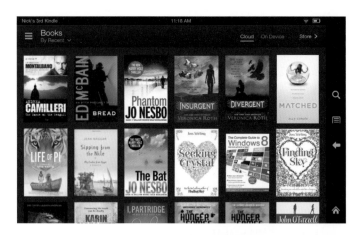

3 Swipe in from the left-hand side to access the menu and tap on the **Kindle Lending Library** link under the **Shop** heading

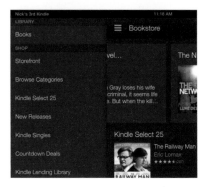

4 Tap on a title to view details about it

Movies and TV shows are provided by the Prime Instant Video service.

5 Tap on the **Borrow for Free** button to download the title to your Kindle Fire

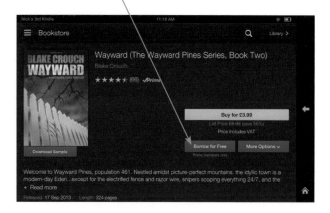

6 Amazon Prime also offers free streaming of a range of movies and TV shows, from the Amazon website

Accessing Menus

Some apps, particularly the built-in Kindle Fire ones that comes pre-installed on your device, have their own menus that can be used for a variety of functions. They are different depending on each app but they can be accessed in the same way:

 Tap on the **Menu** button, in the top left-hand corner of the app's screen (this is either black or gray, depending on the app) or

2 Swipe inwards from the left-hand side of the screen

Tap on a menu item to view it. This could take you away from the current app, i.e. into the Settings app. To get back to the original app, tap on the **Back** button.

3 The menus differ for each app. Hide the menu by tapping on the Menu button again or swiping the menu to the left

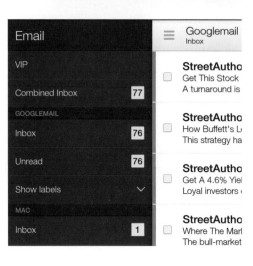

2 Getting Started

The Kindle Fire is, literally, a very hands-on experience. This chapter shows how to quickly get to grips with the interface and controls of your Kindle Fire so that you can begin accessing, managing and using the wide range of available content and the Kindle Fire settings.

The Carousel

After the Kindle Fire has been turned on, and the Lock Screen opened, the first thing you will see is the Home screen. This is in the format of a Carousel with a line of icons for accessing various apps and libraries:

 Swipe left and right to move between items on the Carousel. The most recently-opened item is displayed at the left-hand side of the Carousel

Don't forget

Tap on an item on the Carousel to open it. This can be in any position; it does not have to be the last used app, or the one magnified in the middle of the screen.

 Swipe up on the screen to view the Grid below the Carousel. Change the orientation of the Kindle to view the Carousel and the Grid together

...cont'd

Home recommendations

In portrait mode it is possible to show thumbnail shortcuts to recommended items, beneath the currently active one, i.e. the one being viewed. The type of content in the thumbnails is different for each type of app:

Hot tip

Recommendations can be turned on or off in **Settings > Applications > Home Screen** and tap on the **Show** or **Hide** buttons for Show/Hide Recommendations.

1 Swipe left and right on the Carousel in portrait mode. The currently active icon has shortcut thumbnails underneath it

2 For items such as music, books or apps there will be recommended items underneath the one being viewed

3 Tap on an item to view it, or the tap on the **See all** button to see the full range of related recommendations

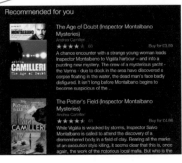

4 For items such as Email or the web browser Silk, the thumbnails link to specific functions of the apps, such as opening up a new email to compose

The Grid

The Carousel function is further enhanced with the Grid option. This appears below the Carousel and can be used to pin your favorite and most frequently used apps so that they are easily available from the Home screen. To use the Grid:

1 The Grid is located below the Carousel. Swipe upwards to view the items in the Grid

Don't forget

If you are viewing the Grid, as in Step 2, and then open an app, the Grid view will be the one to which you return when you tap on the Home button, i.e. it will not revert back to the default Carousel view.

2 Swipe to the top of the screen to view all of the Grid items, without the Carousel being visible

3 Items can be added to the Grid, from the Carousel. Press and hold on an item in the Carousel and tap on the **Add to Home** button

Apps can also be added to the Grid, in the same way as in Step 3, from within the Apps section. This can be accessed by tapping on the **Apps** button on the main Navigation Bar.

4 The item is added in the next available space on the Grid

To remove an item from the Grid, press and hold on it so that it is selected and then tap on the **Remove** button. This only removes it from the Grid and it is still available in the Apps section on your device.

Navigation Bar

The Navigation Bar at the top of the Home screen contains links to all of the main content libraries on the Kindle Fire. To use this:

1 Swipe left and right to view all of the library headings

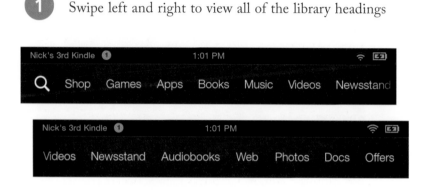

2 Tap on a link to go to that library

The content libraries on the Navigation Bar are:

● **Shop**. This takes you to the Amazon website where you can buy and download content for your Kindle Fire.

● **Games**. This section contains the games that are stored on your Kindle Fire. If more games are downloaded they will be located here.

● **Apps**. This is where your Kindle Fire apps are located and where new apps can be downloaded to.

When viewing a library, tap here to sort it by different criteria.

- **Books**. This section stores the Kindle books that you have downloaded. You can also view books that are not on your Kindle yet, but stored in the Amazon Cloud. When you access them in the Cloud they are automatically downloaded onto your Kindle Fire.

- **Music**. This section contains the music that you have bought from Amazon, or downloaded from your own computer.

The Amazon Prime Video service may not be available in all geographic locations.

- **Videos**. This is where you can access, download and view videos from the Amazon Prime Video service.

- **Newsstand**. This is where you can download newspapers and magazines and take out subscriptions for the latest editions.

- **Audiobooks**. This section has a range of books that can be listened to on your Kindle. It is also possible to access audiobooks from Audible.

- **Web**. This accesses the web, using the Kindle Fire's own web browser, Silk.

- **Photos**. This is where you can view photos that have been uploaded to the Amazon Cloud Drive, or copied to your Kindle Fire.

- **Docs**. This is where you can use documents that have been uploaded to the Amazon Cloud Drive, or copied to your Kindle Fire.

- **Offers**. This is where you can view offers from Amazon. These are the items that also appear on the Lock Screen.

Options Bar

The **Options Bar** appears at the bottom of the screen in portrait mode and the right of the screen in landscape mode. Its two main elements are the Home button and the Back button.

Home button

When you are navigating around the Kindle Fire, it is important to be able to get back to the Home screen as quickly as possible. This is done by tapping on the Home button, which appears on the **Options Bar**, which is on every screen apart from the Home screen. The Home button takes you directly back to the Carousel.

Don't forget

The Options Bar is not physically on the Kindle Fire: if it is not visible within an app, tap on the screen to display it.

 In landscape mode the Home button is located at the bottom of the Options Bar

 In portrait mode the Home button is located at the left-hand side of the Options Bar

Tap on the **Home** button to go back to the Home screen at any point

Back button

Another element on the Options Bar is the Back button. It is used to go back to the previous viewed item or screen. To use the Back button:

1 The Back button is located in the middle of the Options Bar in both landscape and portrait mode

2 Tap on the **Back** button to go back one step. If you are at the start screen of an app or a library this will take you back to the Home screen

3 From within a library item or one of the Kindle Fire Settings, tap on this button to go back up one level

Quick Switch

The Quick Switch option enables you to access items that you have recently used. To do this:

1 Swipe over the Options Bar, upwards in portrait mode, or from right to left in landscape mode, to reveal the Quick Switch panel. Tap on an item to open it, or swipe left and right to view other items

Don't forget

To close the Quick Switch panel, swipe down, or across, on the two bars above, or to the side, of the apps.

Status Bar

The Status Bar is displayed along the top of the Kindle Fire's screen and is visible all of the time.

The Status Bar contains various items, including:

- Your Kindle Fire's friendly name

- The current time

- The status of your Wi-Fi connection (and Bluetooth if used)

- The charge status of the battery

Tap on the **Clear All** button to remove the list of current Notifications.

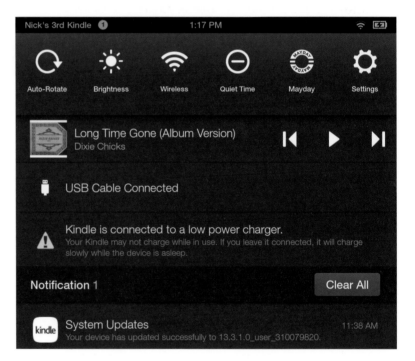

Additional settings can also be accessed from the Status Bar, by swiping downwards from any point on it. This displays the Quick Settings (see next page), Notifications and an option for accessing additional Kindle Fire Settings (see pages 34-39).

Quick Settings

When the Status Bar is expanded, by swiping down on it, the Quick Settings are available below the items on the previous page. These are:

- **Auto-Rotate**. This can be used to Lock/Unlock screen rotation for when you move your Kindle Fire between portrait and landscape mode.

- **Brightness**. This changes the screen brightness. (The lower the screen brightness, the less battery power will be used). Tap on the Brightness button and drag the slider to adjust the screen brightness.

- **Wireless**. Use this to access settings for connecting to and managing Wi-Fi and Bluetooth connections.

- **Quiet Time**. If this is turned on then any notifications on your Kindle Fire will not make any sound (see pages 40-41).

- **Mayday**. This is the online video call help for your Kindle Fire HDX (not available on the HD models). It connects you to a member of the Amazon support staff who will go through any problems that you have with your Kindle Fire and they can even take remote control of your device (see page 47).

- **Settings**. Use this to access the full range of Kindle Fire Settings (see pages 34-39).

Tap on one of the Quick Settings to turn them on or off or to access options for editing them.

Kindle Fire Settings

The Settings button on the Quick Settings Bar provides access to the full range of Kindle Fire Settings. Tap once on the **Settings** button to access them:

The Kindle Fire Settings are:

- **Sync All Content**. This updates any items that have been used on other Amazon devices, or the Amazon website, i.e. if you are reading a book on another device, it will be synced to the latest point on your Kindle Fire.

- **My Account**. This displays information about the registered user including their name and the Kindle email address that would have been created when the Kindle Fire was registered during setup. It also has options for managing your social networking accounts, such as Facebook and Twitter, and also email accounts and contacts.

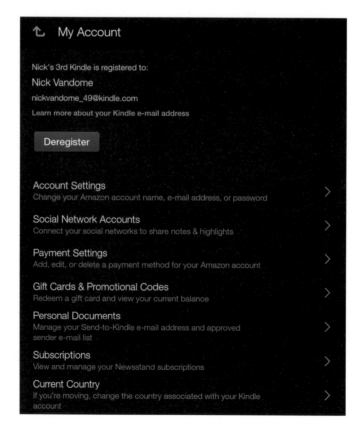

- **Help**. This offers some information about using your Kindle Fire and also access to the Kindle Mayday service.

The Mayday service is a help function that provides a live video link with a member of the Amazon Customer Service staff. You can see them but they cannot see you.

- **Parental Controls**. This can be used to restrict access to certain apps or types of content on the Kindle Fire and also set up new profiles for children, using Kindle FreeTime, with access to specific apps only (see Chapter 12 for more information about this).

...cont'd

- **Device**. This displays information about your Kindle Fire, including the amount of storage that specific items are taking up, the amount of battery power left, a Date & Time option where you can edit your time zone, disable the installation of apps from unknown sources and resetting your Kindle to its factory settings (if you do this you will lose all of your personal data from your Kindle Fire).

Tap the **Show Battery Percentage in Status Bar** button **On** to display the amount of battery power that is left as a percentage.

- **Wireless**. This contains options for managing your Bluetooth and Wi-Fi connections and also for adding new wireless networks.

...cont'd

- **Applications**. This contains a range of functions for managing the applications on your Kindle Fire (see Chapter Five for more information about this).

![Applications settings screenshot]

- **Notifications & Quiet Time**. This can be used to specify times when your Kindle does not make any noise when there are notifications within your apps. See pages 40-41 for details.

![Notifications & Quiet Time settings screenshot]

By default, the Kindle Fire makes a sound when a notification is received, such as an email. Quiet Time can be used to disable this, as can turning down the system volume with the volume buttons.

...cont'd

- **Display & Sounds**. This can be used to set the volume on your Kindle Fire, specify sounds for notifications, set the screen brightness and the screen timeout, i.e. how long before the screen goes to sleep if the Kindle Fire is inactive.

Don't forget

For more details about using the keyboard, see Chapter Three.

- **Language & Keyboard**. This contains options for changing the language used on the Kindle Fire and the format for the keyboard.

...cont'd

- **Accessibility**. This provides a range of settings for users with visual or motor issues. It includes a Screen Reader that reads out text, a Screen Magnifier and Explore by Touch.

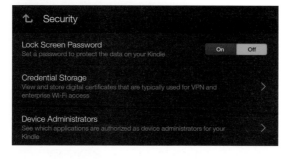

- **Security**. This includes some advanced security settings and also an option for adding a password to the Lock Screen.

- **Legal & Compliance**. This contains details of legal, safety and privacy information.

Quiet Time and Notifications

Several apps on the Kindle Fire are dynamic, which means that they display messages and updated information as and when it becomes available. These include apps such as Email, Skype, system updates and social networking apps including Facebook and Twitter. When notifications for these apps occur they appear in the Notification Tray and a sound also plays. This can become annoying if you are doing something that benefits from peace and quiet. Therefore, the Quiet Time function is a good option for turning off notification sounds at certain times. To do this:

All Notifications must have the same sound assigned to them. This is done in **Settings > Display & Sounds > Notification Sound**.

 Swipe down from the top of the screen and tap on the **Settings** button

 Tap on the **Notifications & Quiet Time** button

Notifications & Quiet Time

 Tap on an app to select its notification options

 Tap the buttons **On** or **Off** to select whether notifications are shown in the Notification Tray or by a sound, or both

Tap on the **Quiet Time** button in Step 3

6 Tap the **Quiet Time** button **On** to enable Quiet Time and Tap on

the **Schedule Quiet Time** button to set specific times for this and tap on the From button

7 Select a time period for when you want Quiet Time to apply and tap on the **Set Time** button

8 In Step 6, check on each option for which you want to enable Quiet

Time, i.e. when you are watching a movie

9 Swipe down from the top of the screen to access the Quick Settings Quiet Time button

10 Tap on the button so that it turns orange to turn Quiet Time **On** and apply the settings made in Steps 6, 7 and 8

If you activate Quiet Time for a specific purpose, remember to turn it off again once this has finished.

41

The Lock Screen

The Kindle Fire can hold an extensive amount of information and data and some of it may be confidential so you will not want everyone having access to it. To ensure that your information is only seen by you, the lock screen can be set with a password that is required before it is unlocked. To apply this:

 The Lock Screen appears when the Kindle Fire is left inactive for a period of time, or when it is put to sleep pressing the **On/Off** button once

Hot tip

The advertisements that appear on the Lock Screen can be disabled, for a fee, when you buy your Kindle Fire.

 Swipe the padlock icon to the left to unlock the screen

...cont'd

3 To set a password for the Lock Screen, swipe down from the top of the screen and tap on the **Settings** button

4 Tap on the **Security** button

Security   >

5 By default, the **Lock Screen Password** is **Off**. Tap on the **On** button to set a password

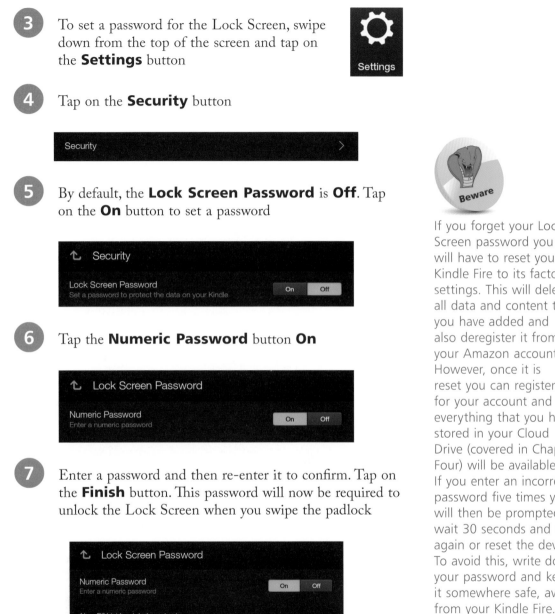

6 Tap the **Numeric Password** button **On**

7 Enter a password and then re-enter it to confirm. Tap on the **Finish** button. This password will now be required to unlock the Lock Screen when you swipe the padlock

Beware

If you forget your Lock Screen password you will have to reset your Kindle Fire to its factory settings. This will delete all data and content that you have added and also deregister it from your Amazon account. However, once it is reset you can register for your account and everything that you have stored in your Cloud Drive (covered in Chapter Four) will be available. If you enter an incorrect password five times you will then be prompted to wait 30 seconds and try again or reset the device. To avoid this, write down your password and keep it somewhere safe, away from your Kindle Fire.

43

Screen Rotation

The Kindle Fire screen can be rotated between portrait and landscape and it offers a slightly different screen view for each mode.

By default, this happen automatically whenever you rotate the screen in your hands. However, there may be times when you want to disable this feature so that the screen is locked in either portrait or landscape mode. To do this:

Hot tip

Locking screen rotation can be a good option when you are reading a book or watching a movie so that the screen does not rotate accidentally if you move the screen slightly.

44

 Access the Status Bar. By default, this button will display **Auto-Rotate**

 Tap on the button so that is displays **Locked**. Repeat the process to unlock screen rotation

3 If the screen is locked, content does not move when the screen is rotated

Searching your Kindle Fire

As you acquire more and more content, it is important to be able to search over your Kindle Fire to find what you are looking for. Searches can be performed over the Kindle Fire's libraries, the Amazon Store or the web. To do this:

1 On the Home screen, in landscape mode, tap on this button (this is also available from the same Options Bar as the Home button and the Back button)

2 On the Home screen, in portrait mode, the Search box appears above the Navigation Bar

3 Tap in the **Search** box

4 Enter a search keyword. Matches will be displayed below the Search box. There will also be options to view Amazon Store and web suggestions

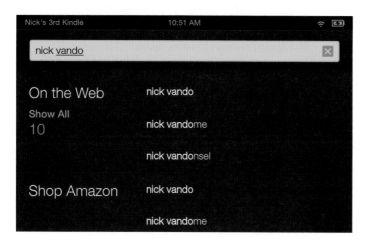

...cont'd

 Tap on the **Show All** button in Step 4 to see a fuller range of the search results

 Tap on one of the results to view it in it default app

7 Web results will be displayed in the default browser and search engine (Silk and Bing respectively). Tap on one to go to that web page

Mayday and Help

Having text Help files on tablets, or links to web pages, is fairly standard and these are available on the Kindle Fire. However, in addition to this, the Help function is taken to a new level with the Mayday option which enables you to have a live video chat with a real person, who will guide you through whichever issue you have. They can also take control of your Kindle Fire and show you what to do through remote control.

To use Mayday and the other Help functions on the Kindle Fire:

 Swipe down from the top of the screen and tap on the **Mayday** button

 The Help pages provide access to the Mayday function. This requires an active Wi-Fi connection

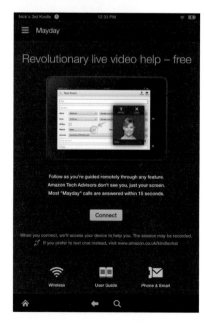

> The Help pages and Mayday can also be accessed from **Settings > Help**.

> When you connect to Mayday, you can see the member of the support staff, but they cannot see you.

 Tap on the **Connect** button to have a video chat with a member of the Amazon support staff

...cont'd

General Help

The same page from which Mayday can be accessed can also be used to access the Kindle Fire User Guide and customer service help via email or phone. To use these:

 Tap on the **User Guide** button to access this on your Kindle Fire. Tap on a link to go to that section in the guide

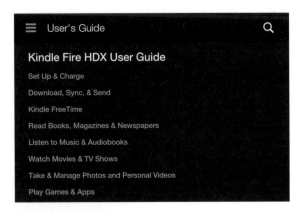

 Tap on the **Phone & Email** button to access the Customer Service options

Tap on the **Select an issue** box and tap on the **E-mail** or **Phone** buttons to select a method for contacting Customer Service

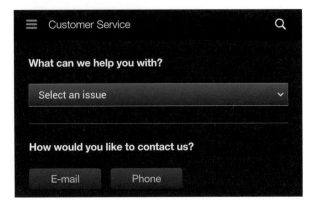

3 Using the Keyboard

The Kindle Fire keyboard is a virtual one that appears on the screen when needed. This chapter shows how to get the most out of the keyboard for adding content.

A Bluetooth keyboard can be bought to use separately from the Kindle Fire HD and HDX. Capacitive stylus pens can also be used to access items on the screen.

Using the Kindle Fire keyboard takes a bit more precision than using a larger, physical, keyboard so you may need a bit of practise to become fully confident with it.

The Kindle Fire Keyboard

The keyboard on a Kindle Fire is a virtual one, i.e. it appears on the touchscreen whenever text or numbered input is required for an app. This can be for a variety of reasons:

● Entering text with a word processing app, email or an organizing app

● Entering a web address

● Entering information into a form

● Entering a password

Viewing the keyboard

When you attempt one of the items above, the keyboard appears before you can enter any text or numbers:

Around the keyboard

To access the various keyboard controls:

1 Tap once on this button to add a single capital letter (the keyboard letters are displayed as capitals)

2 Double-tap on this button to create **Caps Lock**. This is indicated by a orange line underneath the arrow

3 Tap once on this button to back-delete an item

4 Tap once on this button to access the **Numbers** keyboard option

5 From the Numbers keyboard, tap once on this button to access the **Symbols** keyboard

Hot tip

Numbers can also be inserted by pressing and holding on the letters at the top of the standard QWERTY keyboard.

6 Tap once on this button on either of the two keyboards above to return to the standard **QWERTY** option

7 Tap once on this button to hide the keyboard (this can be done from the Navigation Bar at the bottom of the screen). If the keyboard is hidden, tap once on one of the input options, e.g. entering text, to show it again

Keyboard Settings

There are a number of options for setting up the functionality of your Kindle Fire's keyboard. These can be accessed from the Settings section:

1 Swipe down from the top of the screen and tap on the **Settings** app

2 Tap on the **Language & Keyboard** button

> Language & Keyboard

3 Tap on the **Keyboard Settings** button to access the settings for the default keyboard

> **Language & Keyboard**
>
> Language
> English (United States)
>
> Text-to-Speech
> Set the voice for Text-to-Speech applications
>
> Keyboard Language
> Set the language for your on-screen keyboard
>
> Keyboard Settings
> Customize your on-screen keyboard

4 The available settings are shown. Tap the buttons next to each item **On** or **Off** as required

> **Keyboard Settings**
>
> Sound on keypress   On | Off
>
> Auto-correction
> Automatically correct typing mistakes   On | Off
>
> Auto-capitalization   On | Off
>
> Next word prediction
> Predict words based on previously entered text   On | Off
>
> Check Spelling   On | Off
>
> Trace typing
> Enter words by tracing from key to key   On | Off
>
> Personal dictionary
> English

Don't forget

Unless you plan on using a lot of shortcuts in your writing (such as writing in 'text-speak') it is a good idea to turn **On** items such as Auto-correction, Auto-capitalization and Check Spelling.

5 Tap on the **Auto-correction** button to enable the keyboard to offer suggestions to mis-spelled words

6 Tap on the **Auto-capitalization** button to enable the keyboard to automatically insert capital letters at the start of sentence

7 Tap here to enable **Next word prediction** for auto-correction, which helps to make the suggestion in the context of what is being written

8 Tap on the **Check Spelling** button to turn on the spell checker for the keyboard

9 Tap on the **Keyboard Language** button in Step 3 to select a default a language for the keyboard

The language used on your Kindle Fire, and the keyboard, can also be selected when you first set up your device.

Keyboard Shortcuts

Because its size is limited by the size of the Kindle Fire screen, the keyboard cannot display as many keys as a full-sized keyboard. Therefore, the keys double up and have more than one option available. The additional options are accessed by pressing and holding on a key.

1 For keys with numbers above them, press and hold briefly to access the associated number. Tap on the number to insert it

2 Press and hold for slightly longer than in Step 1 to access the full range of options for a key. Tap on the cross to close the options without selecting one

The available shortcut options for each key are (from top to bottom on the keyboard and left to right):

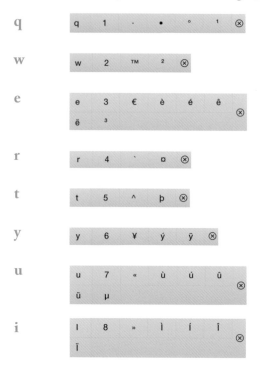

...cont'd

o						
o	9	{	°	ò	ó	⊗
ô	õ	ö	ø	œ		

p				
p	0	}	¶	⊗

a						
a	@	©	ª	à	á	⊗
â	ã	ä	å	æ		

s						
s	$	®	ß	š	§	⊗

d					
d	_	|	ð	¦	⊗

f			
f	(	[	⊗

g			
g	)	]	⊗

h			
h	:	<	⊗

j			
j	;	>	⊗

k			
k	'	&	⊗

l				
l	"	£	"	⊗

z				
z	-	¢	ž	⊗

x			
x	!	¡	⊗

c				
c	#	%	ç	⊗

v			
v	=	*	⊗

b						
b	/	\	÷	¼	½	⊗
¾						

n					
n	+	~	ñ	±	⊗

m			
m	?	¿	⊗

Adding Text

Once you have applied the keyboard settings that you require you can start entering text. To do this:

 Tap once on the screen to activate the keyboard. Start typing with the keyboard. The text will appear at the point where you tapped on the screen

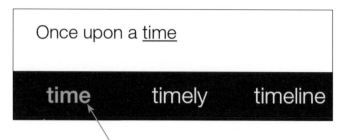

Once upon a time

time   timely   timeline

2   If **Auto-correction** is enabled, suggestions appear above the keyboard. Tap once on the spacebar to accept the suggestion highlighted orange, or tap on another word to insert that instead

3   If the **Spell checker** is enabled, any misspelled words appear underlined in red

Once upon a tyme

tyme   time   thyme

Beware

The Spell checker may not work with all apps that are downloaded from the Appstore. However, these may have their own, built-in, spell checkers instead.

4   Tap on one of the suggestions to replace the misspelled word, or tap on the same suggestion as the word to add it to the dictionary

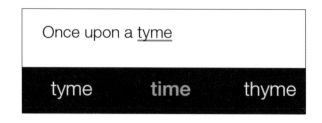

Once upon a tyme

⊕ Add "tyme" to dictionary

...cont'd

Once text has been entered it can be selected, copied, cut and pasted, either within an app or between apps.

Selecting text

To select text and perform tasks on it:

1 Tap anywhere to set the insertion point for adding, or editing, text

Selecting text

2 Drag the marker to move the insertion point

Selecting text

3 Double-tap on a word to activate the selection handles

| Select All | Cut | Copy | Paste |

Selecting text

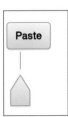

Hot tip

Tap on the **Select All** button to select everything in a document.

4 Drag the handles to change the text that is selected

| Select All | Cut | Copy | Paste |

Selecting text

5 Tap on these buttons at the top of the window to **Cut** or **Copy** the selected text

| Select All | Cut | Copy | Paste |

Selecting text

6 Locate the point at which you want to include the text. Press and hold and tap on **Paste** to add the text

Paste

57

Splitting the Keyboard

For anyone who likes to type with two hands the function for splitting the keyboard on the screen is a useful one:

1 Press and hold on this key on the keyboard

2 Tap on the orange keyboard key

Beware

Splitting the keyboard makes it even smaller and this is best if using it in landscape view.

3 The keyboard is split either side of the screen

4 Reverse the process to return the keyboard to its original state

Voice Typing

If you want to go hands-free for text input, this can be done with the built-in microphone and voice typing function. To do this:

 Tap on this key on the keyboard

2 Speak what you want to appear on screen

Recording

Beware

Voice typing can be a bit hit and miss, so speak as clearly as possible and not too quickly.

3 Tap on the **Done** button

4 The words appear as text on the screen. To add punctuation, speak the items, such as 'comma' or 'question mark'

Hello how are you today
Hello, how are you today?

Personal Dictionaries

When entering text there will be a lot of words that are not recognized by the built-in dictionary. If the spell checker is turned on, these words will be underlined in red. If you want to, these words can be kept and added to your own dictionary so that they are recognized the next time they are used. To do this:

1 Unrecognized words are underlined in red, with options shown below. Tap on the new word to use it

Once upon a tyme

| tyme | time | thyme |

2 Tap on the **Add to dictionary** button to add it to your own user dictionary

Once upon a tyme

⊕ Add "tyme" to dictionary

3 To view the words in your dictionary, select **Settings > Language & Keyboard > Keyboard Settings** and tap on the **Personal dictionary** button

Personal dictionary
English

4 Words that have been added are displayed. These will be recognized when you type them

↱ Personal dictionary

Tyme

Vandome

5 To delete a word, tap here and tap on the **Delete** button

↱ Personal dictionary

Tyme ✓

Vandome

Delete

4 Using Cloud Drive

This chapter shows how to use the online Amazon Cloud Drive to upload your own photos, music and documents and then access and use them through your Kindle Fire.

Accessing the Cloud Drive

As mentioned in Chapter One, the Amazon Cloud Drive can be used to upload content from your computer. Once this has been done, compatible content will be available on your Kindle Fire.

When you buy a Kindle Fire you will automatically be allocated an Amazon Cloud Drive, with 5GB of free storage space. This can then be accessed from your Amazon Account. To do this:

The Amazon Cloud Drive can be used to get content onto your Kindle Fire and it is also an excellent option for backing up your content for safety.

 Access the Amazon website and click on the **Sign in** button to access your Amazon Account with your username and password

 Under the **Your Account** heading, click on the **Your Cloud Drive** link

The Cloud Drive interface is where you can start uploading content from your own computer (see page 67)

Adding Content to the Cloud Drive

The default folders in the Cloud Drive are for, Documents, Pictures, Uploads and Videos. However, these can be deleted or moved and new folders can also be added, using the **New Folder** button. Content can be uploaded to the Cloud Drive Home page or any of the folders. To do this:

1 Click on one of the folders to access it

2 Click on the **Upload Files** button | Upload Files |

You must have an Internet connection to upload files to your Cloud Drive.

3 You will be able to download the Cloud Drive desktop app if you want to upload folders (see pages 64-65)

4 Click on the **Select files to upload** button

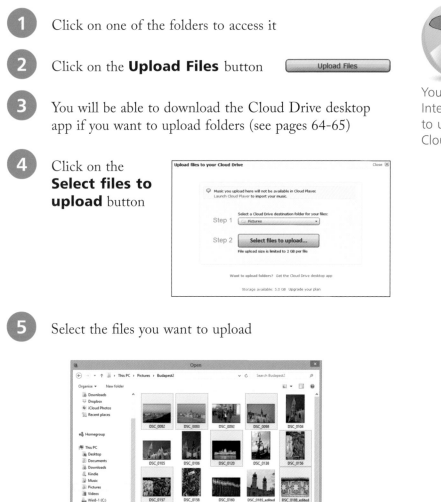

5 Select the files you want to upload

6 Click on the **Open** button. The files will be uploaded to the selected folder in your Cloud Drive

Using the Cloud Drive App

If you want to have a bit more flexibility for uploading folders to your Cloud Drive, rather than just individual files, you can use the Cloud Drive App. This has to be downloaded to your computer and then you can use it to upload your folders to the Cloud Drive. You can also use it for individual files too. To do this:

 When adding content to your Cloud Drive, as on the previous two pages, click on the **Get the Cloud Drive desktop app** button when prompted to download the Cloud Drive App as in Step 3 on page 63

Don't forget

The Cloud Drive App acts like a individual folder within your computer's file structure.

64

 Click on the **Save File** button to save the installation file for the Cloud Drive App

3 Double-click on the installation file once it has been downloaded to install the Cloud Drive app

...cont'd

 4 The Cloud Drive app will be downloaded to your computer and the Set Up Wizard should start

The Cloud Drive App is relatively small in size and should not take very long to download.

5 In the Set Up Wizard, click on the **Next** button

6 You will need your Amazon account details in order to use the Cloud Drive app on your computer. Enter these details and click on the **Sign in** button

65

...cont'd

The Cloud Drive App will create a Cloud Drive folder on your computer, including the files that are already in your Cloud Drive. Click on the **Create my Cloud Drive folder** button

The Cloud Drive on your computer can be accessed from the Amazon Cloud Drive button or directly through your computer's file structure.

The **Amazon Cloud Drive** button is added to your computer. Click on this to open your Cloud Drive folder

Click on the **Cloud Drive** button in your computer's file manager

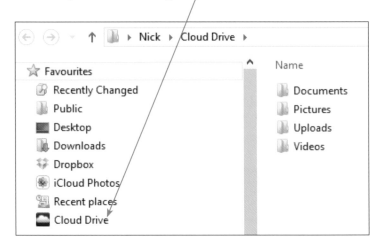

The Cloud Drive folders are displayed. These are the same as on the Amazon website and contain the same content

Uploading Files

Any files can be added to the Cloud Drive, but photos and documents can also be viewed on, and downloaded to, your Kindle Fire.

Although there is a Pictures folder and a Documents folder in the Cloud Drive, photos and documents can be stored anywhere in the Cloud Drive and they will still be available on your Kindle Fire. To add files to your Cloud Drive:

 Click on the **Amazon Cloud Drive** button

 Double-click on a folder within your Cloud Drive file structure

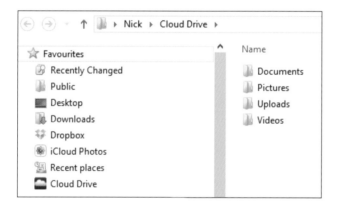

3 Add content to the folder. This can be done by either dragging and dropping it from another location or copying and pasting it

Don't forget

When compatible content is uploaded to your Cloud Drive it will show under the relevant apps on your Kindle Fire, but only under the Cloud heading. Items still have to be downloaded to your Kindle Fire to keep them there. If they are only under the Cloud heading they can be accessed, but only if you have an Internet connection via Wi-Fi.

Viewing Cloud Drive Photos

Once files or folders have been added to your Cloud Drive they can also be viewed on your Kindle Fire. They can also be downloaded to your Kindle Fire, so that you can view them here without being connected to your Cloud Drive. To do this with your Cloud Drive photos:

1 On the main Navigation bar, tap on the **Photos** button

Photos

2 Tap on the Menu button

3 Tap on the **Cloud Drive Files** button to view your files that are stored here

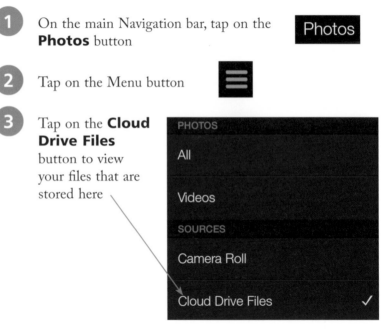

4 The files are displayed in the same folders as in the Cloud Drive on the Amazon website

Videos stored in the Cloud Drive are displayed within folders in the Photos app.

5 Tap on a folder to view all of the items within it

6 Tap on an item in a folder to view it on its own, e.g. a photo at full size

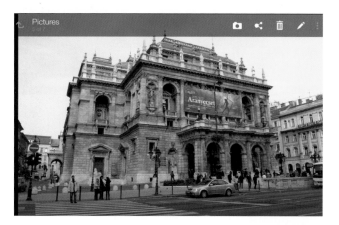

7 Tap on the **Menu** button and tap on the **Download** button to download the open file onto your Kindle Fire, i.e. it will be copied here from the Cloud Drive. It remains in the Cloud Drive too

Beware

If you download a lot of large photos to your Kindle Fire this can start to use up its storage.

Viewing Cloud Drive Videos

Videos stored in the Cloud Drive can also be viewed:

 On the main Navigation bar, tap on the **Photos** button

 The **Videos** folder from the Cloud Drive is displayed within the **Photos** app

Like photos, videos can take up a lot of storage space and they are larger in size than photos.

 Tap on the **Videos** folder to view the items within it

 Tap on a video to view it. This will be played by the video player within the Photos app

Viewing Cloud Drive Docs

Documents stored in the Cloud Drive can also be viewed:

1 On the main Navigation bar, tap on the **Docs** button `Docs`

2 The **Docs** folder is displayed. Tap on the **Cloud** button to view your documents stored in your Cloud Drive

3 Tap on these buttons for more options about adding documents to your Kindle Fire

4 Tap on the **On Device** button to view documents that have been downloaded to your Kindle Fire `On Device`

About Cloud and On Device

The Amazon Cloud plays an important role in the functionality of the Kindle Fire and this is a summary of how the two interact:

- **The Cloud** is used to store all of the content that you have bought from Amazon for your Kindle Fire, e.g. ebooks, music or apps. This can be bought on your Kindle Fire or on the Amazon website. This content can be accessed on your Kindle Fire or the Amazon website, regardless of where it was bought, it is completely interchangeable.

- **The Cloud Drive app** can be used to upload your own content from your computer and stored in your Cloud Drive folder on the Amazon website. You get 5GB of free storage. Photos, videos, books, music and documents can then be downloaded to your Kindle Fire from the Cloud Drive.

Certain libraries have options for viewing content in the Cloud or on the Device, i.e. your Kindle Fire. The ones with this functionality are:

- Apps
- Books
- Docs
- Games
- Music
- Photos

For each item, tap on the **Cloud** or **On Device** buttons at the top of the window to view items in the respective areas. When some items are opened in the Cloud they are downloaded automatically to the Device, while others, such as photos, have to be downloaded manually.

When accessing music in the Cloud, this is streamed to your Kindle Fire via Wi-Fi. If you want to keep it on your device so that you can play it when you are offline, you have to manually download it using the Music app.

Don't forget

For more information about using music on your Kindle Fire, see Chapter Six.

Beware

Music can be streamed via 3G/4G connection, but it is advisable to do it over Wi-Fi if possible as you may encounter data charges for downloading, depending on your data plan.

5 Inspiring with Apps

Apps are now everywhere in the computing world and this chapter looks at working with the apps that are already on the Kindle Fire and shows how to find and download more from the Appstore, including those for playing games.

About Kindle Fire Apps

There are two main types of apps that you need to consider in relation to your Kindle Fire:

- **Pre-installed apps**. These are the ones that will be already installed when you buy your Kindle Fire

- **Apps from the Appstore**. This is a large range of free and paid-for apps that you can download from the online Amazon Appstore and use on your Kindle Fire

To view the apps on your Kindle Fire and in the Appstore

Hot tip

Until an app from the Appstore is installed it will only be visible in the Cloud section on your Kindle Fire. When you first tap on it, it will be installed and available under the **On Device** heading too.

1 Tap on the **Apps** button on the top Navigation Bar

2 Tap on the **Cloud** button to view the apps on your Kindle Fire. These include the pre-installed ones and any that you have downloaded from the Appstore

Don't forget

The pre-installed apps are displayed with a tick on them in the Cloud section. When an app is added to the device it is installed from the Appstore and is displayed with a tick too.

3   Tap on the **On Device** button to view the apps that are available on your Kindle Fire. Tap on an app to open it and start using it. These apps will also be available from the Grid on the Home screen

4   Tap on the **Store** button to view the apps that are available on your Kindle Fire. Tap on an app to preview details about it and download it, if required

Pre-installed Apps

Kindle Fire apps are the programs that provide its functionality, whether it is surfing the web, using email or playing games.

Some apps are pre-installed on the Kindle Fire and these include:

- **Calendar**. This can be used to store information about events, and links to any calendars you have with online webmail accounts.

Apps (applications) is just the name that is given to what traditionally has been called computer programs.

- **Camera**. This is a forward-facing camera that can be used for video calls and taking photos.

- **Clock**. A standard clock that can be set for different time zones and also used as an alarm.

- **Contacts**. This is the Kindle Fire address book that can be used to store contacts' details such as name, email and phone number.

- **Email**. This app can be used to link to webmail accounts such as Gmail, Hotmail or Yahoo!. You can also use it to link to an IMAP or a POP3 email account (see pages 150-151).

- **Help**. This contains the Kindle Fire User Guide and also the online help service, Mayday.

- **IMDb**. This is an app that links to a large database of information about movies, TV shows, video games and related information.

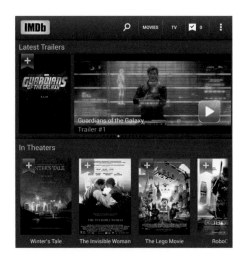

IMDb stands for Internet Movie Database.

- **Kindle FreeTime**. This is the Kindle Fire app for setting up user profiles for children and restricting the content which is available for them.

- **Settings**. This contains a range of settings for the Kindle Fire.

- **Silk**. This is the Kindle Fire web browser.

- **Shop Amazon**. This links to the Amazon Shop where you can download a huge range of content.

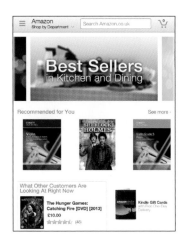

Finding Apps

The pre-installed Kindle Fire apps are a good starting point, but you will soon want to start expanding your app horizons. This is done through the Amazon Appstore. To start using this:

1 Tap on the **Apps** button on the main Navigation Bar

2 Tap on the **Store** button

3 The top panel displays the top free app of the day and other new and popular apps that are being promoted

4 The middle panel displays featured apps. Swipe left and right to view more of these

Don't forget

The apps displayed on the Home screen of the Appstore change on a regular basis so it is worth checking this frequently to see what is new.

5 The bottom panel has recommendations from Amazon, which are based on your previous purchases

6 Swipe left and right on the top panel to view different suggestions and recommendations for new apps

7 Swipe up on the Home screen to view the full range of recommended apps

8 Tap on the **See more** button next to a particular category to view a fuller range of available apps

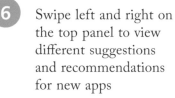

9 Swipe up and down within a category to view the apps

Searching for Apps

There are several options for searching for apps in the Appstore:

1 Tap on the **Menu** button at the top of the Appstore

The Appstore, or Apps, Menu has an option for **Collections**. This enables you to create groups of similar apps which are stored within specific folders. These can then be added to the Home screen by pressing and holding on the folders and tapping on the **Add to Home** button.

2 Tap on the **Browse Categories** button to view all of the different options

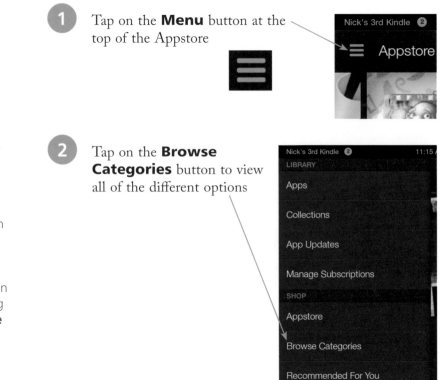

Collections can also be created by dragging one app over another on the Home screen or in the Apps library.

3 Tap on a category to view the apps within it. Within a category, tap on the **All Categories** button

4 The apps for each category are displayed in a similar interface to those on the Home screen. Swipe left or right or up and down to view the available apps

Don't forget

The Search box at the top of the window can also be used for searching for apps by entering a keyword or name of an app.

5 Tap here to refine your search by selecting sections within the main category

Downloading Apps

When you find an app that you want to use on your Kindle Fire it can be downloaded in a couple of taps, providing that you have a Wi-Fi connection to the Internet. To do this:

Beware

Apps can be streamed via 3G/4G connection, but it is advisable to do it over Wi-Fi if possible as you may encounter data charges for downloading, depending on your data plan.

Don't forget

Most apps download in a few minutes at the most, depending on the speed of your Internet connection.

 Tap on an app to view additional details about it

 Tap on this button to download the app (if it is a paid-for app it will display the price)

 Tap on the **Get App** button

 Tap on the **Open** button to start downloading an app

 Once the app has been downloaded and opened it is available in the Apps library under the **On Device** button

Deleting Apps

Apps that have been downloaded can be deleted from your Kindle Fire, in which case they still remain in the Cloud.

1 In the Apps library, tap on the **On Device** button

2 Press and hold on an app that has previously been downloaded

3 Tap on the **Remove from Device** button to delete the app

4 Tap on the **Cloud** button. The deleted app is still available here. Tap on it once to reinstall it, or

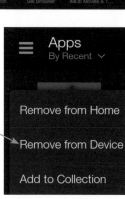

5 Tap and hold on the app and tap on the **Delete from Cloud** button to remove it completely. If this is done the app can still be reinstalled from the Appstore. An app can only be removed from the Cloud if it has first been removed from the Device

Hot tip

Even if you delete an app from the Cloud you will be able to reinstall it, free of charge if it was a paid-for app, from the Appstore.

Amazon Coins

Within the Appstore there is also an option to use Amazon Coins to buy apps (and other content from Amazon via your Kindle Fire, such as books and music). This is a form of virtual currency and the coins can be bought on the Amazon website at a discounted rate compared to using standard currencies to buy items. To use and buy Amazon Coins:

Appstore will display the prices in your local currency, as set in Chapter 1 - UK Pounds in this instance.

 For items in the Appstore, the price is usually displayed in local currency and Amazon Coins. Tap on the price button

£1.99 or 199 coins

 Tap on the radio button next to the Coins value and tap on the **Get App** button

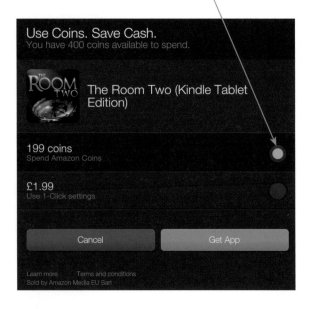

Tap on the **Learn more** button to find out about Amazon Coins on the Amazon website

Learn more

4 Information about Amazon Coins is displayed, including how to buy, earn and redeem them. (Coins can be used directly on the Amazon website as well as through the Kindle Fire)

5 When you have coins, the number is displayed at the bottom of the page when you want to buy something. Tap here to buy more

85

Hot tip

The greater the number of coins that you buy, the greater the discount.

6 Select the number of coins that you want to buy and tap on the **Buy** button

Games Apps

Games are a popular pastime on the Kindle Fire and there is a range of games apps in the Appstore that will keep users entertained for hours. To use these:

 Tap on the Games button on the main Navigation Bar

 Any games that you already have are shown here. Tap on the **Store** button to go to the Games section of the Appstore

Tap on the Games section **Menu** to view more options for finding games apps.

 Navigate for free, paid-for and recommended games apps in the same way as for other items in the Appstore, by swiping left and right and up and down. Tap on a games app to view details about it

4 Tap on the **Get App** button to download a game

5 Games apps include digital versions of popular board games like Monopoly, Chess and Backgammon

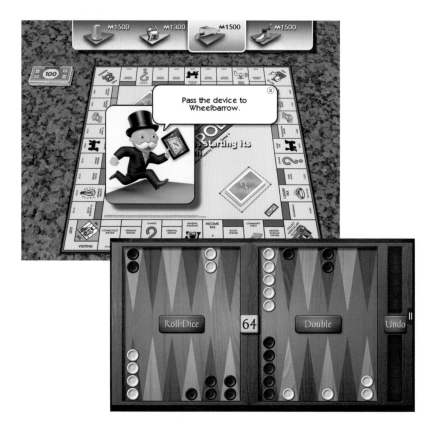

Hot tip

Tap on the Profile button on the Games Menu to create a GameCircle profile for sharing your scores in games with other GameCircle members. Some games can also be played directly with other GameCircle members.

87

Apps Settings

Within the Kindle Fire Settings there are a number of options for working with and managing your apps.

 Swipe down from the top of the screen to access the Status Bar and tap on the **Settings** button

 Tap on the **Applications** link

Applications >

The Applications section has a number of options including: notification settings for when apps need to display updated information, details about installed apps (see next page), syncing your Kindle Fire content with your Amazon Cloud content and information relating to the pre-installed Amazon apps such as those for reading audiobooks and playing music

Applications

Apps from Unknown Sources
Allow installation of applications that are not from Appstore   On   Off

Collect App Usage Data
Allow Appstore to collect information on the frequency
and duration of use of downloaded apps.   On   Off

Manage All Applications   >

AMAZON APPLICATIONS

Amazon GameCircle   >

Appstore   >

Audiobooks   >

Camera   >

Email, Contacts, Calendars   >

Home Screen   >

Music   >

Photos   >

Hot tip

Under the **Applications** link, tap on the **Home Screen** link to access settings for turning off recommendations from appearing below the Carousel in portrait mode.

4 Tap on the **Installed Applications** link in Step 3 to view detailed information about all of the apps on your Kindle Fire. These are not just the apps that appear in the Apps library but all of those on the device

5 Tap on an app to view its full details, including how much space it is taking up and the permissions that the app has for accessing other items. Tap on the **Force Stop** button if the app has frozen or stopped working

6 If it is an app that has been downloaded from the Appstore, tap on the **Uninstall** button to remove it from your Kindle Fire

Some Apps to Consider

Everyone has their own ideas about which apps are essential to them, depending on their interests and priorities. However, these are some apps that may be of interest:

- **Angry Birds**. The bestselling Internet game, now available in a Kindle Fire version.

- **Calculator Plus Free**. A simple but functional calculator.

- **Candy Crush**. Another hugely popular game that involves matching lines of similar colored pieces of candy.

- **Drawing Pad.** A drawing app for creating your own artwork.

- **Fruit Ninja**. A simple, but fun, game that consists of slicing different types of fruit with a sword.

- **HD Battery**. This is an app that can be used to monitor the battery usage of your Kindle Fire and view how long you can use it for different functions.

- **Hill Climb Racing**. A compelling game where you have to drive different vehicles up and down challenging terrains.

- **How to Draw: All Lessons**. A versatile and comprehensive drawing app that offers lessons and tutorials for a wide range of drawing projects.

- **K-pop Karaoke**. Sing along to your favorite tunes with this karaoke app.

- **King of Maths**. A game that is also a learning aid. Advance through the medieval social scene by answering maths questions and solving puzzles.

- **Smart Writing Tool**. An app for creating text with your own handwriting.

- **Temple Run**. A popular game that involves running through a ruined temple, avoiding various obstacles.

- **TuneIn Radio**. Use this to listen to a range of radio stations on your Kindle Fire.

- **Zoom Challenge**. A fun game where you have to guess various objects just from a zoomed-in photo.

6 Music and Video

The Kindle Fire is a great device for providing digital entertainment and this chapter looks at using music and video. It details options for getting music onto your Kindle Fire and then shows how to use it once it is there.

Launching the Cloud Player

Playing music is one of the most popular activities on a tablet and the Kindle Fire provides this functionality with the Music library for storing and playing music. It also links to the Cloud Player for uploading music from your own computer to the Cloud Drive, from where it is then made available to your Kindle Fire. To use the Cloud Player:

 Log in to your Amazon account and select **Your Account > Your Cloud Player**

 The Cloud Player has a similar interface to the Cloud Drive. Click on the **Import your music** button

You have no music stored in your Amazon Cloud Player.

Your plan has space for 200 songs.

Import your music

or

Shop for music in the Amazon MP3 Store
All purchases are stored for free.

amazonMP3 store

 You will be prompted to download the Amazon Music Importer. This can be used to upload your music to your Cloud Player. Click on the **Download Now** button and follow the installation instructions

Get the Amazon Music Importer

The Amazon Music Importer finds your songs and playlists from iTunes, Windows Media Player, or your computer's music folders, and allows you to add them to Cloud Player with a single click. Learn more.

Installation Instructions

The Amazon Music Importer requires Adobe AIR which will be installed automatically if it is not already on your computer.

1. Click **Download now** below to install the Amazon Music Importer.
2. When prompted, select **Save File**.
3. Double-click **AmazonMusicImporterInstaller...exe** in your browser's Downloads window.

Download Now   Cancel

4 Click on the **Save File** button to save the Music Installer installation files

> Opening AmazonMusicImporterInstaller-2.1.0._V37101766... ✕
>
> You have chosen to open:
>
> 🖹 **AmazonMusicImporterInstaller-2.1.0._V371017662_.exe**
>
> which is: Binary File (9.2 MB)
> from: https://images-na.ssl-images-amazon.com
>
> Would you like to save this file?
>
> [Save File] [Cancel]

5 Enter a name for your computer and click on the **Authorize Device** button to enable the Music Importer to recognize where it is installed

Don't forget

The spellings displayed by the Kindle Fire are determined by your Language settings, as covered on page 38. In this illustration, the spellings are in UK English.

93

6 Click on the **Amazon Music Importer** button on your computer and log in with your Amazon account details

Amazon Music Importer

Don't forget

Unlike the Amazon Cloud Drive app, the Music Importer does not show up in your computer's file structure and can only be accessed from the button in Step 6.

amazon music importer

Sign in to your Amazon account to import your music
E-mail address:
Password:
Sign in ►
Forgot your password?

Uploading Music

The Amazon Music Importer can be used to upload music from your computer, either automatically by scanning your iTunes, Windows Media Player or Music folders, or you can select files manually. To upload music to the Cloud Player using the Music Importer:

Beware

The Amazon Music Importer does not support DRM (Digital Rights Management) AAC files, which are often used in iTunes. These files will have to be converted into another format, for example, MP3, before they are uploaded by the Music Importer.

 Access the Music Importer as shown in Step 6 on the previous page

 The Music Importer window has options for scanning your computer or browsing for files

 Click on the **Browse manually** button

 Browse to the music files that you want to import and click on the **OK** button, or select a folder and click on the **Select Folder** button

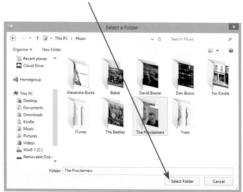

5 To find music automatically with the Music Importer, click on the **Start scan** button in Step 2

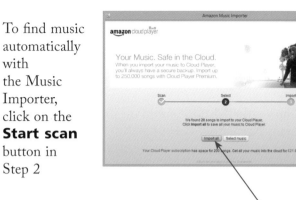

6 The Music Importer will scan over your music content and indicate compatible files for uploading. Click on the **Import all** button

Don't forget

Music can also be bought and downloaded to your Kindle Fire from the Amazon MP3 Store.

95

7 The music is added to the Cloud Player (you can upload 250 songs for free to the Cloud Player). Click on the **Close** button

8 Click here to view your music by specific criteria

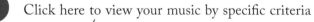

Transferring Music

Music in the Cloud Player can be played on your computer but it can also be downloaded to your Kindle Fire so that you can take it with you wherever you are. To do this:

Hot tip

Music can also be transferred by connecting your Kindle Fire to your computer with the supplied cable and copying music files into the Kindle Fire's **Music** folder.

Beware

Music can be transferred via 3G/4G connection, but it is advisable to do it over Wi-Fi if possible as you may encounter data charges for downloading, depending on your data plan.

 Tap on the **Music** button on the main Navigation Bar

 Tap on the **Cloud** button. This displays the items that have been uploaded to your Cloud Player

3 Tap on an item to view it. Songs can be played directly from the Cloud, but this requires a Wi-Fi Internet connection

4 Tap on the **Download All** button to download all of the songs in a specific album, or

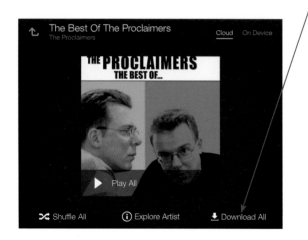

5 Press and hold on a song and tap on the **Download** button to download it to your Kindle Fire

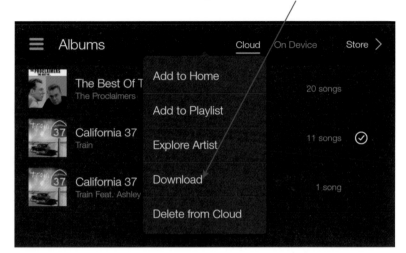

6 Tap on the **On Device** button to view items that have been downloaded onto to your Kindle Fire

Music that is just stored in the Cloud and not downloaded to your Device will only play on your Kindle Fire if you are connected to the Internet via Wi-Fi.

7 Once an item has been downloaded to your Kindle Fire it appears with a tick next to it in the **Cloud** section

Managing your Music

Once music has been downloaded to your Kindle Fire you can start to organize, and play your audio collection.

The Music app's Menu can also be accessed by swiping inwards from the left-hand side of the screen.

 Tap on the **Music** button on the main Navigation Bar

 Tap on the **On Device** button to view the items in your Music library

 Tap on this button to access the Music app's **Menu**

4 Tap on an item on the menu to view items in the Music app according to different criteria, such as by **Songs**

 At the bottom of the Menu are options for adding more music to the Library, Settings and Help

Creating a Playlist

Within the Music library it is also possible to create playlists, i.e. collections of your favorite songs for specific purposes, such as creating a playlist for a party. To do this:

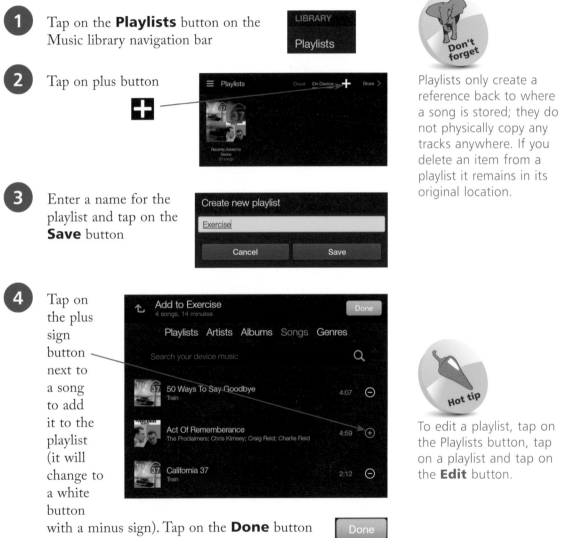

1 Tap on the **Playlists** button on the Music library navigation bar

LIBRARY

Playlists

2 Tap on plus button

3 Enter a name for the playlist and tap on the **Save** button

Create new playlist

Exercise

Cancel   Save

4 Tap on the plus sign button next to a song to add it to the playlist (it will change to a white button with a minus sign). Tap on the **Done** button to finish adding songs

Add to Exercise
4 songs, 14 minutes   Done

Playlists Artists Albums Songs Genres

Search your device music

50 Ways To Say Goodbye
Train   4:07

Act Of Rememberance
The Proclaimers; Chris Kimsey; Craig Reid; Charlie Reid   4:59

California 37
Train   2:12

Done

5 Tap on the **Playlists** button to view available playlists. Tap on a playlist's name to play it. Press and hold on the playlist's name and tap on the **Edit** button to add or delete songs

Don't forget

Playlists only create a reference back to where a song is stored; they do not physically copy any tracks anywhere. If you delete an item from a playlist it remains in its original location.

Hot tip

To edit a playlist, tap on the Playlists button, tap on a playlist and tap on the **Edit** button.

Playing Music

Within the Music library there are a number of options for playing music on your Kindle Fire.

1 Tap on an item in the Music library (if it is an album it will display all of its songs)

The Music Player is part of the Music app, i.e. it is self-contained within the app.

2 Tap on a song to play it in the Music Player

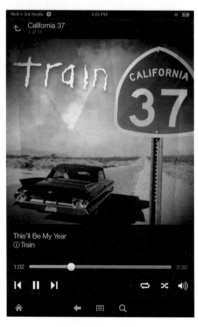

3 Use these buttons to, from left to right, go to the start of the song, play/pause the song, go to the end of the song

4 Drag this slider to increase or decrease the volume

1:31 ● 3:30

5 Tap on this button so it turns orange to **Shuffle** the order in which songs are played

6 Tap on this button so it turns orange to play the current song, or album, on **Repeat**

7 Tap this button to adjust the **Volume** of the tracks playing on the Music Player

8 Tap on the **Menu** button on the Options Bar and tap on the **Clear Player** button to stop the current song and remove it from the Music Player

⊗ Clear Player

9 When a song is being played you can leave the Music Player and view other areas on your Kindle Fire and the song will continue. It will also be displayed in the **Notifications** area. To see this, swipe down from the top of the screen. The currently-playing song is displayed, along with the playback controls

101

The playback controls in the Notifications area can be used to Play/Pause a song or go to the beginning or end of it.

Viewing your own Videos

There are two main options available for viewing videos on your Kindle Fire:

- Download your videos from your computer, or a removable drive

- View movies and TV shows

To view your own videos:

 Copy the video to your computer or insert a memory card with the video on it (this should be in MP4 format)

 Connect your Kindle Fire with the Micro-B/USB Connector cable. Open the Kindle Fire's **Internal storage**

▲ 📱 Kindle
  ▷ 💾 Internal storage

 Navigate to the **Movies** folder in your Kindle Fire's file structure. Double-click on it to open it

📁 Movies
   File folder

 Copy the video file into the **Movies** folder. Other videos can be copied here too but if they are in an incompatible format, e.g. Windows Media Video (WMV) they will not be visible on your Kindle Fire

▶ Computer ▶ Kindle ▶ Internal storage ▶ Movies

...cont'd

5 Tap on the **Photos** button on your Kindle Fire's main Navigation Bar

6 Compatible videos will be displayed in the app

Your own videos can also be accessed from the **Videos** button on the main Navigation Bar. Tap on the **Menu** button and swipe down the menu and tap on the **Personal Videos** button.

7 Press and hold on a video to access options for deleting it (**Delete** button) and viewing file information about it (**Info** button)

8 Tap on a video to play it in the Photos app

Viewing Movies and More

If you want to watch commercial movies and TV shows this can be done through a subscription service provided by Amazon for this type of content. This is the Amazon Prime Instant Video service that can be accessed in two ways: the full Amazon Prime service, or the Amazon Prime Instant Video service, rather than the full Prime service (UK).

Amazon Prime and Prime Instant Video

In the US and UK, the Amazon Prime service can be used to stream and watch movies and TV shows, using the Prime Instant Video element (Amazon Prime also provides free delivery on Amazon purchases and a free lending library for books). This costs US $99/year and UK £79/year *(correct at the time of printing)* and the Kindle Fire has to be located in the US/UK and the user must have a US/UK credit card. In the UK, the Prime Instant Video service can also be used on its own, without having to subscribe to the full Prime service. This costs £5.99/month.

Using Prime Instant Video

To access and stream movies and TV shows on your Kindle Fire:

Streaming video means that it is played over the Internet and so you need an active Internet connection for this.

 Tap on the **Videos** button on the main Navigation Bar

If you just subscribe to the Prime Instant Video service in the UK, it is only a few pounds more annually to upgrade to the full Prime service.

The Prime Instant Video interface displays new and recommended titles. Tap on an item to view its details and, in a lot of instances, view a trailer of the movie or TV show

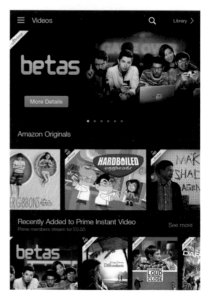

104

3 Tap on the **Watch** button to start viewing the item. If you stop viewing it, you can access it again and start from the point at which you left off

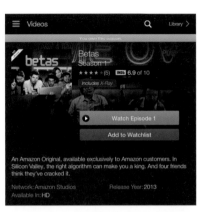

In the UK, the Prime Instant Video service replaces the video service that was previously provided by LOVEFiLM. As LOVEFiLM is an Amazon company this is just essentially a renaming of the service.

4 Tap on the **See more** button in Step 2 to view items according to the main **Movies** or **TV** headings

5 Tap on the **Menu** button at the top of the **Videos** window

6 Tap on these buttons to view specific categories within Prime Instant Video

Beware

Videos can be streamed via 3G/4G connection, but it is advisable to do it over Wi-Fi if possible as you may encounter data charges for downloading, depending on your data plan.

Issues with Video

Although you can watch a wide range of video content on your Kindle Fire there are still some issues associated with this:

● When watching movies or TV shows from Prime Instant Video the content is streamed to your Kindle Fire. This means that it is sent to your Kindle Fire as you are watching it, over a Wi-Fi connection. The advantage of this is that it is a more efficient use of the bandwidth of the Wi-Fi, but the disadvantage is that you have to be in range of a Wi-Fi connection in order to watch the content.

● Since the Kindle Fire supports a limited number of video file formats (MP4 and VP8) some video files will not play on your Kindle Fire. This could include your own home videos and also any commercial movies that you have copied to your computer. One option for overcoming this is to use a video encoder to convert your videos into a Kindle Fire compatible format (MP4 is the best option). Video encoders are programs that convert one video file format into your selected one. There are dozens of these programs available on the web, for Windows and Mac. Some are free, while others have to be paid for. Enter 'video encoders' into a web search engine to find a list of current options.

● The Kindle Fire web browser, Silk, does not support Flash, so it will not play Flash video content on the web. However, this is becoming less of an issue than it would have been a few years ago as fewer websites are relying on Flash, as Adobe, its maker, is no longer developing Flash for mobile devices. But it is still a consideration to bear in mind if you need to use Flash. Amazon has developed an experimental streaming viewer to view Flash content from a limited number of websites and this may appear when accessing items from these sites. The viewer converts the Flash content into a format that can be used with the Silk browser and it can be streamed to your Kindle Fire, i.e. you have to watch it while you are connected to the Internet.

7 Clicking with Photos

The high quality screen of the Kindle Fire is ideal for displaying photos and this chapter shows how to obtain, view, share and edit them.

Photos on the Kindle Fire

There are a number of ways that photos can be added to the Kindle Fire:

- From the Cloud Drive via the Amazon website

- From the Cloud Drive app on your computer

- Directly from your computer via USB cable

- With the Kindle Fire's camera

Uploading online with Cloud Drive

To upload photos from the Amazon Cloud Drive:

 Click on the **Pictures** folder

 Click on the **Upload Files** to select photos from your computer

Uploading with the Cloud Drive app

If the Cloud Drive app has been downloaded to your computer, this can be used to add photos.

 Click on the **Amazon Cloud Drive** button on your computer

 Drag, or copy and paste, photos into the **Pictures** folder within the Cloud Drive file structure

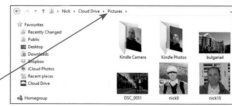

Don't forget

When photos have been added via the Cloud Drive website or the Cloud Drive app, they are visible from the Cloud through the Photos app on the Kindle Fire, but they have to be downloaded to place them here permanently

Uploading from your computer

Photos can also be uploaded directly from your computer to your Kindle Fire:

 Connect your Kindle Fire to your computer using the supplied USB cable (which can also be used for charging)

 Select the Kindle Fire in the computer's file manager

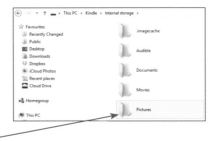

 Click on the **Pictures** folder and drag, or copy and paste, photos into this folder

Capturing with the camera

The camera on the Kindle Fire is a front-facing one that is best used for video calls. However, it can still be used to take photos that can be viewed in the Photos app.

 Tap on the **Camera** app

 Tap on this button to take a photo

 Tap on these buttons to toggle between photo and video mode

Hot tip

Press the **Up** volume button to zoom in on a subject with the camera.

Around the Photos App

Photos, and videos, can be viewed, managed and edited in the Photos app. To do this:

1 Tap on the **Photos** button on the main Navigation Bar

2 Tap on the **Menu** button to access the Photos app main menu. By default, the view is for **All**

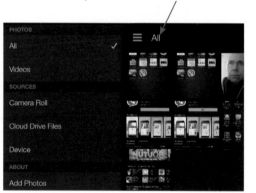

To download a photo that is stored in the Cloud Drive but not on the Kindle Fire, press and hold on it and tap on the **Download** button.

3 Tap on the **Videos** button to view videos rather than photos

4 Tap on the **Camera Roll** button to view photos you have captured with the Kindle Fire's camera

5 Tap on the **Cloud Drive Files** button to view photos you have captured with the Kindle Fire's camera

...cont'd

6 Tap on the **Device** button to view photos that have been downloaded to your Kindle Fire, or been captured with the camera

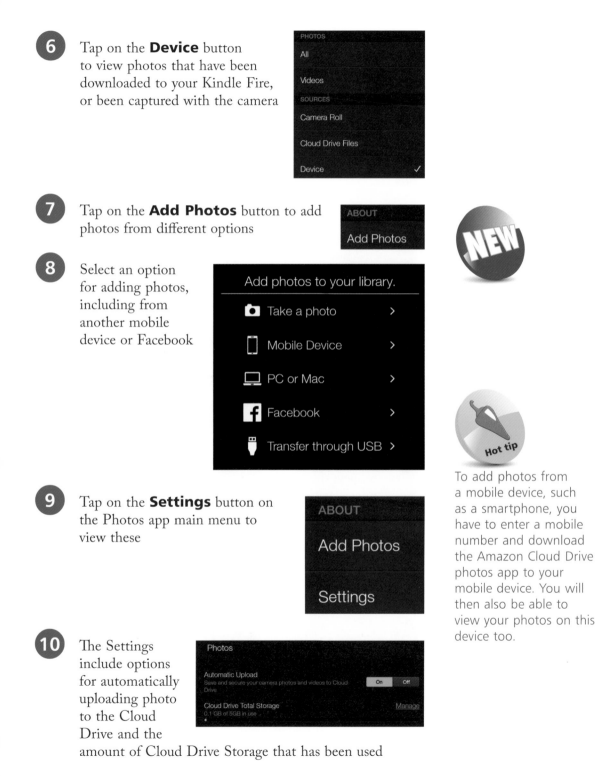

PHOTOS

All

Videos

SOURCES

Camera Roll

Cloud Drive Files

Device ✓

7 Tap on the **Add Photos** button to add photos from different options

ABOUT

Add Photos

8 Select an option for adding photos, including from another mobile device or Facebook

Add photos to your library.

📷 Take a photo >

📱 Mobile Device >

💻 PC or Mac >

f Facebook >

🔌 Transfer through USB >

9 Tap on the **Settings** button on the Photos app main menu to view these

ABOUT

Add Photos

Settings

10 The Settings include options for automatically uploading photo to the Cloud Drive and the amount of Cloud Drive Storage that has been used

Photos

Automatic Upload
Save and secure your camera photos and videos to Cloud Drive
On Off

Cloud Drive Total Storage
0.1 GB of 5GB in use
Manage

NEW

Hot tip

To add photos from a mobile device, such as a smartphone, you have to enter a mobile number and download the Amazon Cloud Drive photos app to your mobile device. You will then also be able to view your photos on this device too.

111

Viewing Photos

Photos in the Photos app are stored in separate folders and they can be viewed from within these.

 By default, all photos in the Photos app are displayed

 Select an option from the Photos app menu, such as **Device**, to view the available folders

 Tap on a folder to view the photos within it, in thumbnail format

Hot tip

The **Back** button on the **Options Bar** can also be used to go back up one level within the Photos app.

 Tap on the folder name at the top of the screen to move back up a level to view all folders again

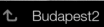

5 Tap on an individual photo to view it at full size

Hot tip

Swipe outwards with thumb and forefinger to zoom in on a photo. Pinch inwards to zoom back out. Zooming in and out can also be done, to a lesser degree, by double-tapping with one finger.

6 If a photo has been taken in landscape mode, rotate the Kindle Fire so that the photo can utilize more of the screen area

Hot tip

Depending on what other apps you have installed, the **Share** option in Step 7 can also be used to convert a photo to PDF or print it using a dedicated printing app.

7 Use these buttons on the top toolbar to, from left to right, access the camera to take a photo, share the current photo, delete the current photo, edit the current photo and access its menu

Selecting Photos

Photos can be selected within a folder and then be printed or deleted. To do this:

1 Tap this button on the top toolbar when viewing photos in a folder

2 Tap on each of the photos that you want to select

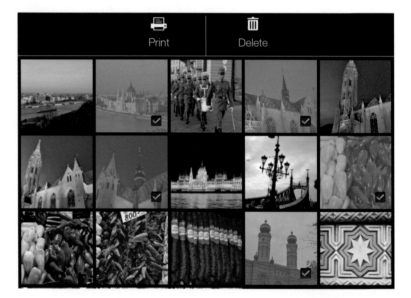

3 When a photo is selected it appears grayed-out with an orange tick on it

4 Tap on the **Print** or **Delete** buttons on the top toolbar of the folder to apply either of these functions

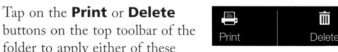

Beware

Printing items from your Kindle Fire can be more difficult than from a traditional computer. The Appstore has a number of printing apps and some work better than others. Some are for specific printers while others are generic. In all cases you will require a wireless printer that is compatible with printing from a Kindle Fire.

Sharing Photos

With the expansion of digital photography, and the number of devices on which to view digital photos, it is now more important than ever for mobile devices to be able to share photos. On the Kindle Fire this can be done through the Photos app:

 Open a folder and tap on the **Share** button on the top toolbar

Tap on the photos you want to share, in the same way as selecting them on the previous page

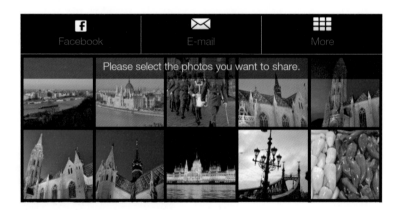

Tap on the options for sharing, including to your Facebook page and by email

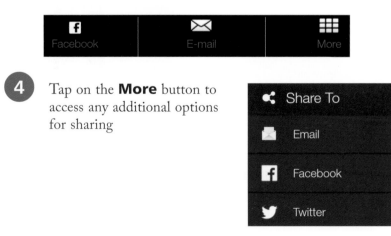

Tap on the **More** button to access any additional options for sharing

Editing Photos

The Photos app has a range of editing functions that can be used to crop photos, enhance the color, rotate and add filters, stickers and text. To edit your photos:

 Open a photo at full size

When photos are edited, the edited version is saved as a copy and the original is untouched.

 Tap on the **Edit** button on the top toolbar

 The photo is displayed with the editing toolbar along the bottom of the screen

If a copy of an edited photo does not appear in the folder immediately, go up one level and then back to the folder to see if the copy is there.

Tap on each button to apply that editing effect

5 Tap on the **Enhance** button to activate options for adjusting the overall colors in the photo

6 Tap on the **Crop** button and drag the resizing handles to remove unwanted areas in a photo. Tap on the options at the bottom of the screen to crop the photo proportionately

Most photos benefit from some cropping, to highlight the main subject and remove any unwanted elements in the background.

7 Tap on the **Rotate** button and tap on the appropriate button to rotate the photo to the left or right, or flip it horizontally or vertically

...cont'd

Don't forget

Filters can be used for a range of effects and can be a good option for creating a number of different artistic styles for the same photo.

8 Tap on the **Redeye** button and select a brush size to tap on any redeye that appears in a photo

9 Tap on the **Filters** button and tap on one of the filter options at the bottom of the screen to apply that effect to the photo

10 Tap on the **Stickers** button and tap on one of the stickers options to add it to a photo. The stickers can be dragged around and resized within a photo

11 Tap on the **Text** and **Meme** buttons to add text to a photo. Tap on the buttons at the bottom of the screen to select a text color. Drag the text box to move and resize it.

(The Meme options enables you to add text headings and footers on a photo)

12 Tap on the **Draw** button to draw on the photo. Tap on the circles at the bottom of the screen to select a pencil size and color

Unlike some photo editing apps, the options in Step 13 do not have an Auto function; all of the effects have to be applied manually.

13 Tap on the **Brightness, Contrast, Saturation, Warmth** and **Sharpness** buttons to edit these features

Drag the slider to apply differing levels for each item.

...cont'd

14 Tap on the **Blemish** and **Whiten** buttons to remove slight blemishes in a photo or enhance the whiteness of people's teeth. For each, select a brush size and tap on the required area

Hot tip

The Focus option is an excellent way to emphasize part of photo while blurring the rest. It is a technique commonly deployed by photographers when capturing photos.

120

15 Tap on the **Focus** button to select an area of the photo to remain in focus while the rest is blurred (also known as depth of field)

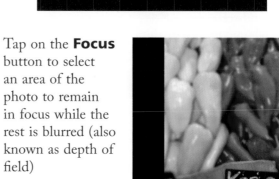

16 Tap on the **Splash** button to select an area that is shown in its original color while the rest of the photo is black and white. Tap on the **Free Color** button at the bottom of the screen and drag on the photo

17 Tap on the **Done** button to apply each editing effect after it has been added

8 A Passion for Reading

The Kindle Fire continues the reading tradition of the original Kindle and this chapter looks at obtaining books and how to navigate your way around them and share your own thoughts and opinions with the online Kindle book community.

Obtaining Books

Amazon started life as an online bookseller and there is an unsurpassed range of content for the Kindle Fire here. Books are stored and accessed from the Books library, from where you can also access the full range of Kindle books on the Amazon website. (Magazines and newspapers can be accessed in a similar way, using the **Newsstand** button.)

Don't forget

Kindle books are usually less expensive than the hard copy versions.

Kindle books are also known as eBooks, which stands for electronic books.

122

Hot tip

To delete a book from your library, select it in the **On Device** section. Press and hold on its cover and tap on the **Remove from Device** button. The book can then be downloaded again from the Store, for free, if required.

 Tap on the **Books** button on the main Navigation Bar

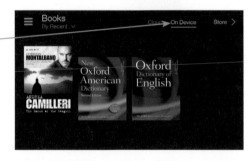 Tap on the **On Device** button to view the books that you already have on your Kindle Fire

 Tap on the **Cloud** button to view all of the books that you have downloaded, including those downloaded on other devices. The ones that have already been downloaded to your Kindle Fire are denoted with a tick

4 Tap on a title in the **Cloud** to download it to your Kindle Fire, where it appears under the **On Device** button with a **New** tag on it

5 Tap on the **Store** button to go to the online Amazon Kindle Store

6 Navigate through the Store using the main panels, or

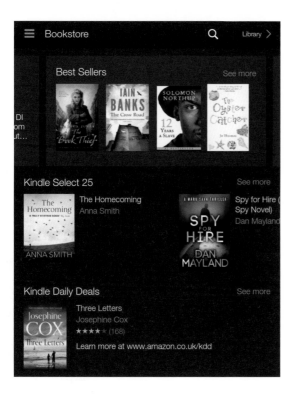

Hot tip

If you have the Kindle app on other devices you will have the same titles available on your Kindle Fire and vice versa.

...cont'd

 7 Tap on the **Menu** button

 8 Tap under the **Browse Categories** heading to view books in these specific categories

LIBRARY

Books

Collections

SHOP

Storefront

Browse Categories

Kindle Select 25

9 Tap on a category to view the books there

≡ Bookstore

Browse Kindle Books

Arts and Photography

Biographies & True Accounts

Business and Finance

Children's Books

Comics and Graphic Novels

Don't forget

The Amazon Kindle Bookstore has a huge range of titles so you should never be short of something to read.

10 Tap on a title to view more details about it. Tap on the **Download Sample** button for a free sample or the **Buy** button to purchase the book

Hot tip

It is always worth downloading a sample for a book, if there is one, in case you decide that you don't really like it and don't want to download the full title.

11 Swipe down the page to view a description of the book and any titles that other people have also bought as well as the current book

12 Swipe further down the page to view product details about the book, such as its sales rank on Amazon and print length

Book Settings

With hard copy books there is very little flexibility in terms of changing the type of paper or the size of the text. However, with a Kindle book you have a range of settings that you can change and customize.

Don't forget

Tap on the left-hand or right-hand edge of a page to move to the previous or next one, or swipe left or right from the edge.

Beware

If you tap too close to the edge of the page to access the Settings or Location Bar you may turn the page instead. Make sure you tap in the middle of the page to avoid this.

1 Open a book and tap in the middle of a page

2 Tap on the **View** button

3 Tap on one of the **Font Size** buttons to make the text larger or smaller

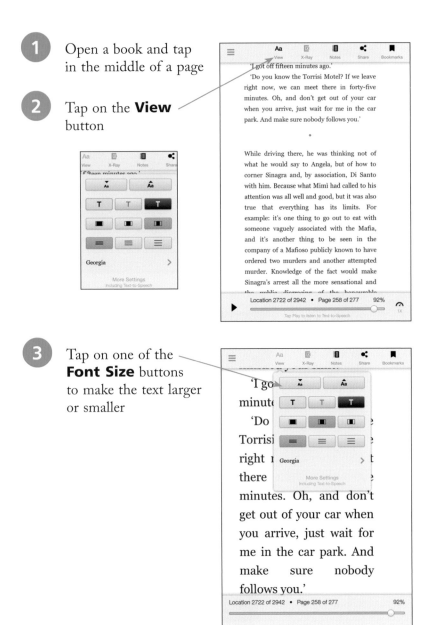

...cont'd

4 Tap on one of the **Color Mode** buttons to use black text on a white background, a sepia background, or white text on a black background

5 Tap on one of the **Margins** buttons to specify how much space appears around the text

Don't forget

Unlike the original Kindle, the Kindle Fire has an LCD screen which means that it is backlit and makes it brighter for reading. Some people prefer this, while others prefer the original.

Reading Aloud

The final option in the Settings section is for the Text-to-Speech function with Kindle books. If this is enabled, books with this functionality can be read aloud by your Kindle Fire. To do this:

Beware

The voice for the Text-to-Speech option is not very realistic and can be irritating after a period of time of reading.

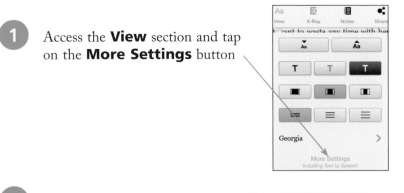

1 Access the **View** section and tap on the **More Settings** button

2 Tap on the **On** button next to **Text-to-Speech**

3 Tap in the middle of a page to access the bottom Location Bar. If it has Text-to-Speech functionality this is denoted by a **Play** button at the left-hand side of the Location Bar

4 Tap on the **Play** button to start the Kindle Fire reading the book. This is done with a computer-generated voice and so is more monotone than if it were being read by an actual person

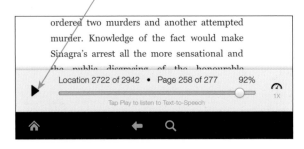

Thumbing Through Books

A common concern with eBooks is that you will lose your place and not be able to find it again. However, Kindle books have great flexibility for navigating around so that you can quickly move to specific points in your book including pages and locations.

1 Tap on the **Menu** button

2 Swipe up and down to access specific chapters

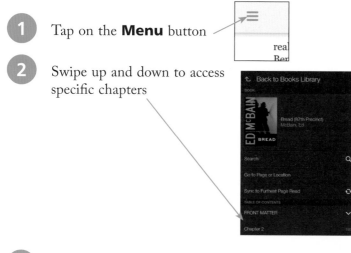

3 Tap on this button to sync the book with any copy of the same book that you are reading on another device

Sync to Furthest Page Read

4 Tap on this button to go to a specific location

Go to Page or Location

5 Enter the location or page number and tap on the appropriate button

Enter page (1 - 277) or location (1 - 2942)
You are currently at page 258, location 2722.
205
Cancel   Page   Location

6 Not all Kindle books have page numbers. For those that do, this is indicated in their **Product Details**. If there is a **Page Numbers Source ISBN** this means that the Kindle book has page numbers that correspond to the hard copy

Product Details
Sales Rank:
#65 Paid in Kindle Store
Language: English
Print Length: 183 pages
Page Numbers Source ISBN:
1477818502

Don't forget

The Location Bar at the bottom of the screen displays the location and page numbers. The location numbers are specific to individual lines of text to make it easier to locate items.

Adding Notes and Bookmarks

If you like taking notes while you are reading books you no longer have to worry about jotting down your thoughts in the margins or on pieces of paper. With Kindle books you can add your own electronic notes and also insert bookmarks at your favorite passages. To do this:

1 Tap and hold to activate the magnifier icon and drag it over text to highlight it

2 Tap on the **Note** button

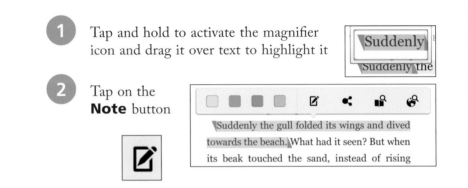

Don't forget

The color for highlighted text can be selected in Step 2 by tapping on one of the colored buttons.

3 Enter the note that applies to the selected text and tap on the **Save** button

Page 3 - Note

Bird details and information.

Cancel   Save

4 A note is indicated by a small blue icon next to the highlighted text. Tap on this to view details of the note

had something changed in the natural order? Suddenly the gull folded its wings and dived towards the beach. What had it seen? But when its beak touched the sand, instead of rising

5 To view all of your notes, tap in the middle of a page and tap on the **Notes** button

6 Notes and highlighted text are shown on the **My Notes & Marks** page. Tap on an item to go to that point in the book

Highlighted text and notes are displayed separately in the **Notes** section.

Adding bookmarks

1 To bookmark a page in a book, tap in the top right-hand corner. Tap again to remove it

THE DANCE OF THE SEAGULL (INSPECTOR MONTALBANO MYSTERIES)

wouldn't know what the hell to reply.

'Just right now I can't, Mr Commissioner.'

'Listen, Montalbano, I am ordering you—'

'I just got a call from the hospital telling me that Fazio, my man, has regained consciousness and wants to see me . . .'

'Then come to my office immediately after you see him.'

2 Bookmarks are included on the **My Notes & Marks** page. Tap on a bookmark to go to that location

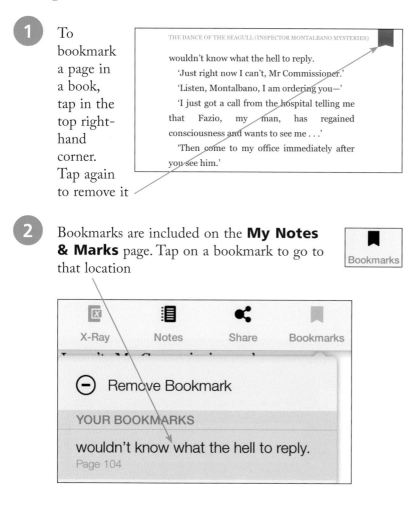

X-Ray Notes Share Bookmarks

⊖ Remove Bookmark

YOUR BOOKMARKS

wouldn't know what the hell to reply.
Page 104

Sharing your Thoughts

Reading Kindle books can be a very collaborative experience: you can easily share passages and your thoughts and opinions with social networking sites and see what other people have to say about the books they are reading.

1 Highlight a piece of text

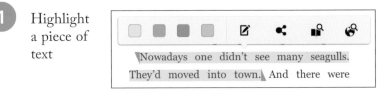

2 Tap on the **Share** button. If you do not add any comments, just the highlighted text will be shared

3 Comments can be entered to accompany the hightlighted text. This is optional

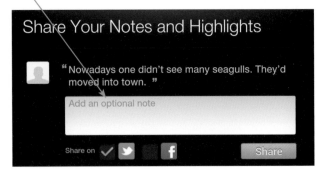

4 Enter any comments as required. Select a site where you want to share the content and tap on the **Share** button

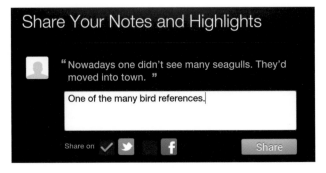

Don't forget

You can share text and comments with a compatible social networking site, such as Facebook or Twitter, if you have an account with these services.

Finding Definitions

One of the great things about reading is that we not only get a lot of enjoyment from it, but also learn new things. Kindle books are excellent for expanding our vocabularies, without having to resort to looking up a separate dictionary. This is done with the definition feature:

1 Press and hold on a word to see a quick definition for it

2 Tap on the **Full Definition** link in Step 1 to see a more extensive explanation of the word

3 Swipe to the left to view a Wikipedia entry and also a translation option for the word

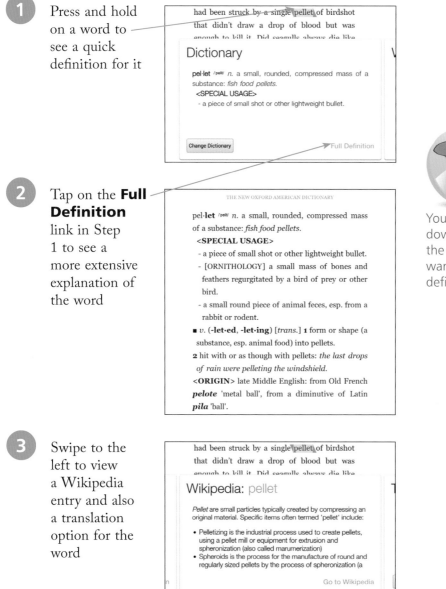

You may be prompted to download a dictionary the first time that you want to look up a definition for a word.

Turning on the X-Ray

The X-Ray feature for books on the Kindle Fire can be used to view the 'bare bones' of a page, chapter or book. This highlights characters, locations or terms, provides additional information about them, if applicable, and shows where they occur at specific locations.

Beware

Not all books have the X-Ray functionality.

1 Tap in the middle of a page and tap on the **X-Ray** button

X-Ray

2 The people, places and terms are listed on the X-Ray page. The more blue lines next to an item, the more entries it has

X-Ray
By Relevance ∨   ✕

All 49   People 37   Terms 12

Current Page

👤 Oscar Hemmings
   " "This guy Oscar Hemmings. The third guy in Diamondback
   Development." "Oh, yes," Carella said. "

👤 Charlie Harrod
   " His name was Charles Harrod, and his address was 1512
   Kruger Street. The listing was significant only in that
   Diamondback was the city's largest black ghetto. "

👤 Alfred Allen Chase
   " "Alfred Allen Chase," the amber-eyed man said.
   "Robinson Worthy," the man with the glasses said, and
   put down the gasoline-station pictures and shifted the... "

3 Tap on an entry to see fuller details about it and examples of where it appears in the chapter or in the book

↰ Charlie Harrod   ✕

" His name was Charles Harrod, and his address was 1512
Kruger Street. The listing was significant only in that
Diamondback was the city's largest black ghetto. "

Chapter 5

His name was Charles Harrod, and his address was 1512 Kruger
Street. The listing was significant only in that Diamondback was the
city's largest black ghetto.
Loc 788

Only one of them had a name in the space provided, and the name
was not Charles Harrod's.
Loc 824

Magazines

In addition to books, magazines can also be download to, and read on, your Kindle Fire. To do this:

 1 Tap on the **Newsstand** button on the main Navigation Bar

Newsstand

2 Browse for magazines in a similar way as for books. Tap on a thumbnail to view details about it

3 Tap here to obtain the magazine. It can be read on your Kindle Fire in a similar way as for a book

Beware

Most magazines are displayed as being Free. However, this is usually just for a sample and if you want to buy the full magazine, or subscribe to it, then you will have to pay a fee.

Audiobooks

For anyone with visual issues, or who just prefers listening to books, there is an audiobooks service where books can be downloaded and then narrated on your Kindle Fire. To use this:

 Tap on the **Audiobooks** button on the main Navigation Bar

 Audiobooks

2 Navigate the **Audiobooks Store** in the same way as for the Books Store

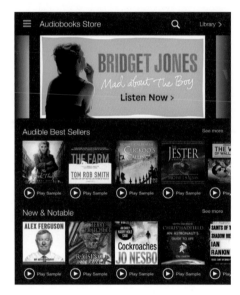

Audiobooks usually have a real person as the narrator and so are much better to listen to than a computer-generated voice.

136

3 Tap here to listen to a sample and tap on the **Buy** button to purchase the full version

9 Bringing the Web to Life

On the Kindle Fire the Web is accessed through the Silk browser. This chapter introduces using Silk and covers popular browsing issues such as using tabs, navigating around the Web, bookmarking pages and working with links and images on websites.

Browsing on the Kindle Fire

Web browsing is an essential part of everyday life and the Kindle Fire provides this with its own web browser, called Silk. This provides a fast, fluid browsing experience with its own interface and settings. To use Silk to access the web:

Beware

There are limited options in terms of using other web browsers on the Kindle Fire and so it is probably best to stick to the Silk browser.

138

 Tap on the **Web** button on the main Navigation Bar, or

 Tap on the **Apps** button on the main Navigation Bar and tap on the **Silk** app

 Press and hold on the Silk app and tap on the **Add to Home** button to add it to the Grid underneath the Carousel on the Home screen

 Tap on the **Silk** app to open the browser

Getting Silky

The Silk browser has a slightly different interface to the ones that many people may be used to from using desktop and laptop computers, but most of its functionality is similar. To use the Silk browser:

① Access the Silk browser as shown on the previous page. The first page that appears is the **Starter** page. This contains a list of **Most Visited** sites. This is also the page that appears when a new tab is opened in the Silk browser

② Swipe in from the left-hand margin to view the Silk controls and settings

Opening Pages

Web pages can be opened directly from the Starter page, either from the thumbnails or by entering a web address or search word into the Search/Address box at the top of the browser.

Don't forget

Since Silk is designed and optimized for the Kindle Fire it usually opens web pages quickly and efficiently.

Hot tip

Once web pages have been opened, content can be zoomed in on by swiping outwards on the screen with thumb and forefinger. Pinch inwards with thumb and forefinger to zoom back out again on a page.

 On the Starter page, tap on one of the thumbnails under the **Most Visited**. These will change as you visit different websites

Swipe in from the left of the page and tap on the **History** or **Trending Now** options

Tap in the **Search/Address** box. Previously-visited pages are shown underneath. Tap on one to go to that page, or

Enter a website address or search word into the box. As you type, suggestions will appear. Tap on one to go to a list of search results and tap on one to go to that page

Finding your Way Around

The navigation in the Silk browser is mostly done through the Kindle Fire's **Options Bar**, which appears along the border of the browser.

 Tap on the **Menu** button on the Options Bar to access options for sharing a page with other people via email or social media, adding a bookmark to the page, finding specific words or phrases on a page or requesting another page view, e.g. mobile or standard view (see page 145)

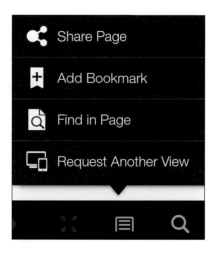

(see page 145)

The **Find in Page** option can be a good one for finding items on long web pages or ones that contain a lot of text.

 Tap on these buttons to move forwards and backwards through pages that you have already visited (these are just for the Silk browser, not the Kindle Fire Back button for returning to the previous item)

 Tap on this button to view the current web page at full screen. This hides the Options Bar and the Tabs Bar at the top of the screen. Swipe upwards on this button to return to standard view

Bookmarking Pages

The favorite pages that you visit will show up in the **Most Visited** section on the **Starter** page. It is also possible to bookmark pages so that you can find them quickly. To do this:

1 Open the page that you want to bookmark and tap on the **Menu** button at the bottom of the screen and tap on the **Add Bookmark** button

2 Tap in the **Name** box and enter a name for the bookmark. Tap on the **OK** button

3 To view bookmarks, access the Starter page menu, as shown in Step 2 on page 139, and tap on the **Bookmarks** link

Hot tip

To remove a bookmarked page, press and hold on it within the Bookmarks section and tap on the **Delete** button.

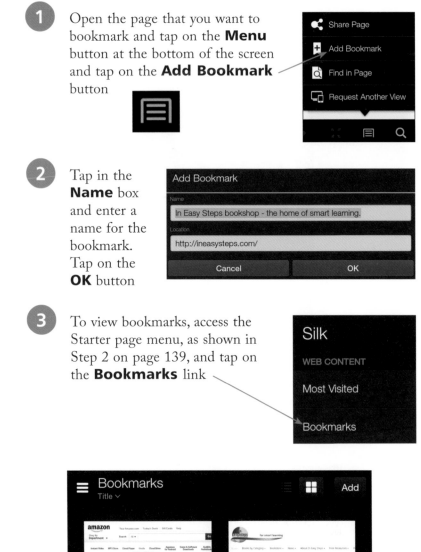

Links and Images

Links and images are both essential items on websites: links provide the functionality for moving between pages and sites, while images provide the all-important graphical element. To work with these:

1 Press and hold on a link to access its menu (tap once on a link to go directly to the linked page). The options on the menu are for opening the link in the current tab, opening it in a new tab, opening it in a new tab while you remain viewing the current tab (background option), adding the link as a bookmark, sharing it via email and copying it so that it could be pasted into the Search/Address box

Don't forget

On a lot of web pages, images also serve as links to other pages or sites.

143

http://www.bbc.co.uk/news/science-environment-26343894

Open

Open in New Tab

Open in Background Tab

Bookmark Link

Share Link

Copy Link URL

Save Link

2 Press and hold on an image to access its menu. The options are for saving it (into your Photos library) and viewing it on a page on its own

Adding Tabs

The Silk browser supports the use of tabs, whereby you can open numerous pages within the same browser window. To do this:

 Tap on this button at the top right-hand corner of the browser window to add a new tab

 Open a new page from the Starter page or by entering a web address or search word into the Search/Address box

 New tabs are opened at the top of the browser

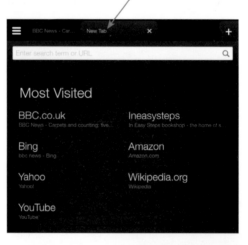

Hot tip

To remove a tab, tap on the white cross at the right-hand side of it.

 Tap and hold on a tab name to view the tab menu with options for closing tabs, adding or removing bookmarks for the current page or sharing it

Changing Page Views

A lot of web browsers for mobile devices, such as Silk, can display web pages in a mobile or a desktop page. The mobile version is optimized for the smaller screen and the desktop version contains more detail. To switch between views:

1 The default view may depend on the settings for individual websites. Desktop view may look rather small and cramped

2 Tap on the **Menu** button at the bottom of the screen and tap on the **Request Another View** button

3 Check on the radio button next to the view which you want to use

Beware

A lot of websites still only have one view, i.e. the desktop one. However, this is changing as more people realize the importance of the mobile world.

4 In Mobile view, items tend to be placed one above another. Scroll up and down to view the items

Viewing the History

To view your Silk web browsing history:

 From any web page, swipe in from the left of the screen and tap on the **History** button

Unlike some web browsers, there is no 'private browsing' option with Silk.

 Recently-visited pages are displayed, grouped according to the time and day on which they were viewed. Tap on the **Clear All** button to delete these items from your History or tap on a cross next to a page to delete it without deleting anything else

☰ History   Clear All

⌄ Today

9:04AM   BBC News - Steven Moffat on the world of Doctor...   ✕
          http://www.bbc.co.uk/news/entertainment-arts-26342072

9:03AM   BBC News - World War One: Eleven shot at dawn in...   ✕
          http://www.bbc.co.uk/news/uk-england-25654341

9:03AM   BBC News - Home   ✕
          http://www.bbc.co.uk/news/

9:03AM   bbc news - Bing   ✕
          http://www.bing.com/search?pc=AMAZ&form=AMAZWB&setm...

8:29AM   In Easy Steps bookshop - the home of smart learning. ✕
          http://ineasysteps.com/

8:29AM   Coming soon | In Easy Steps   ✕
          http://ineasysteps.com/books-by-category/coming-soon/

⌃ Yesterday

Tap on a page in your History to open it in Silk

Using Reading View

The Reader function enables you to read web pages with only the text and not any other content.

1 If a web page has this button on its tab it indicates that the Reader function is available. Tap on it to view the page in **Reading View** format

2 The page is displayed as text only. Tap on the cross in the top right-hand corner to return to standard view

Steven Moffat on the world of Doctor Who and Sherlock

26 February 2014 Last updated at 01:42
By Ian Youngs Entertainment reporter, BBC News

Steven Moffat (centre) was accompanied by Sherlock's Benedict Cumberbatch (left) and Doctor Who's Matt Smith when he received a special Bafta Award

3 In standard view, the **Reading View** button is on a black background

Silk Settings

For the functional side of using Silk, there are several settings that can be accessed to customize the way that the browser works. This is done from the Settings button:

1 On any web page, swipe in from the left of the screen and tap on the **Settings** button

2 The available settings are displayed. Tap on one to view its options. Swipe up to view the full range of settings. Tap on **Search Engine**, to select a default search engine for Silk; and **Block Pop-Up Windows**, which can be used to stop pop-ups on your web pages

Pop-ups are usually in the form of advertisements that appear, unsolicited, as a small window on a web page.

Cached items are those that are temporarily stored by the browser to make the loading of the page quicker the next time that you look at it. You have to refresh the page to see the latest version of a cached web page if it has been updated since the time the cache was taken, e.g. for sports websites.

Cookies are small items from websites that obtain details from your browser when you visit a site. The cookie remembers the details for the next time you visit the site.

3 Tap on the **Clear Browser Data** button to remove items from your browser

Clear Browser Data
History, Cache, Passwords, Cookies or Location Access.

4 Select items such as history, cached items, passwords and cookies and tap on the **Confirm** button if you want to remove them

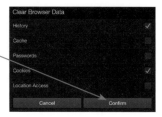

148

10 Keeping in Touch

This chapter shows how to use your Kindle Fire to keep in touch with family and friends using email, address books, calendars and linking to social networking sites.

Adding Email Accounts

Email functionality on the Kindle Fire is provided by the Email app. This is an app that enables you to link to your email accounts (either webmail, IMAP or POP3 accounts) so that you can get all of your emails on your Kindle Fire. To set up email accounts:

Don't forget

Webmail is an email service that is accessed through a web browser, such as Gmail or Hotmail. IMAP and POP3 are protocols for retrieving emails that are stored on a remote server. The emails can be downloaded from here onto your own computer using a separate email client.

 Tap on the **Apps** link on the main Navigation Bar

 Tap on the **Email** app

3 Enter the email address of the account you want to add and tap on the **Next** button

Don't forget

You can add more than one email account via the Email app and get all of your emails in one place.

4 Enter the details of your email account and tap on the **Next** button (this should be a webmail account that you have already set up and are using)

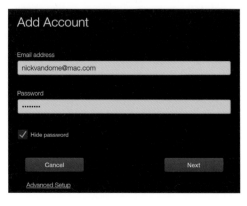

5 Tap on the **Go to Inbox** button to complete the account setup and view the Inbox for this account

6 If the account is not added automatically, tap on the **Advanced Setup** button in Step 3

Advanced Setup

7 Select the type of email account that you want to add and insert the relevant server settings (you may need to get these from the company that provides your email service)

Beware

If you are setting up a POP3 or an IMAP email account (usually non-web based ones) you will need certain settings such as those for the incoming and outgoing servers. These should be available from your email service provider.

Working with Email

Sending an email

Once an email account has been set up, it will be accessed when you tap on the **Email** app.

1 The available accounts will be displayed. Tap here to access the menu options for the account

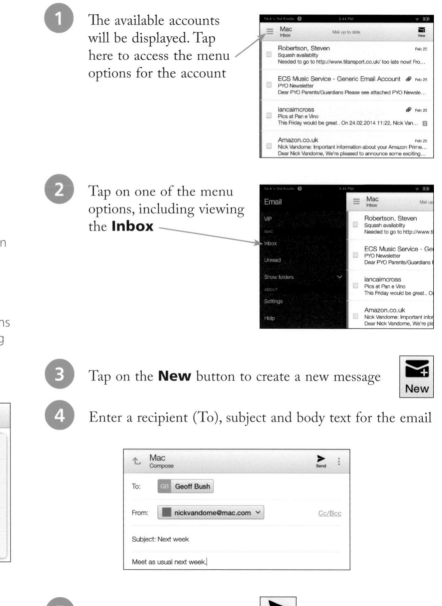

Don't forget

Tap on the Menu button in the top right-hand corner of a new email to access options for attaching items to the email, formatting options and saving or discarding a draft of the email.

2 Tap on one of the menu options, including viewing the **Inbox**

3 Tap on the **New** button to create a new message

New

4 Enter a recipient (To), subject and body text for the email

Mac	Send
Compose	

To: GB Geoff Bush

From: nickvandome@mac.com ⌄   Cc/Bcc

Subject: Next week

Meet as usual next week.

5 Tap on the **Send** button

Send

Email settings

Email settings can be accessed for specific accounts and also general email settings that apply to any account. To apply general settings:

1 In the Email app, tap on the **Menu** button and tap on the **Settings** link

2 Tap on the **Email General Settings** button

Email, Contacts, Calendars

Email General Settings

3 Select options for text size in emails, showing images, downloading attachments automatically and whether to include the original message in a reply

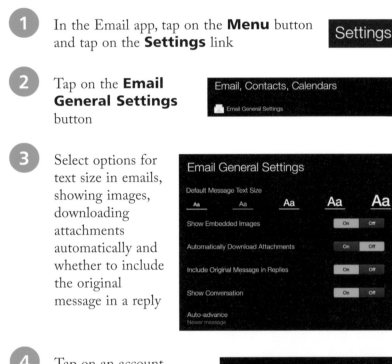

Email General Settings

Default Message Text Size

Aa   Aa   Aa   Aa   Aa

Show Embedded Images   On   Off
Automatically Download Attachments   On   Off
Include Original Message in Replies   On   Off
Show Conversation   On   Off

Auto-advance
Newer message

4 Tap on an account name on the page in Step 2 to view its

Mac (default)
Mac (nickvandome@mac.com)

specific settings. These include options for checking for new emails, adding a signature to emails and the account server settings

Deleting an email account
To delete an email account:

1 Access the settings for an account as in Step 4 above and tap on the **Remove Account** button

nickvandome@mac.com

Your name
Nick Vandome

Description
Mac

SYNC AND DATA SETTINGS

Inbox check frequency
Automatic (push)

Store messages
One month

Signature
Append text to messages you send

SERVER SETTINGS

Incoming settings
Username, password, and other incoming server settings

Outgoing settings
Username, password, and other outgoing server settings

REMOVE ACCOUNT

Delete account from device   Remove Account

Don't forget

If you remove an account you can still add it again at any time.

Adding Contacts

An important part of staying in touch with people is having an up-to-date address book. On the Kindle Fire you can use the Contacts app:

1 Tap on the **Apps** link on the main Navigation Bar

2 Tap on the **Contacts** app

3 Tap on the **Set up my profile** link

Don't forget

To edit a contact's details, access their entry and tap on the **Edit** button.

Edit

4 Enter your contact details, including name, email and phone number and tap on the **Save** button

Save

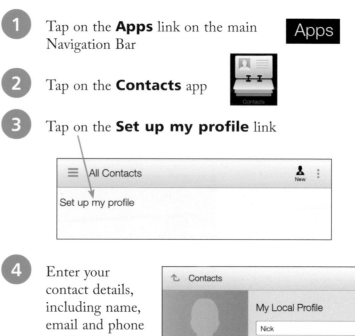

5 Your own profile is added in the Contacts app. Tap on this button to go back to the Contacts app's Home page

6 Tap on the **New** button to add a new contact and enter the information in the same way as for your own profile

New

7 All contacts are displayed alphabetically, based on first name, on the Home page (under your own details). Tap on one to view their details

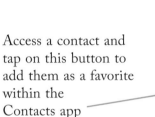

8 Access a contact and tap on this button to add them as a favorite within the Contacts app

Hot tip

In Edit mode, tap on the colored square next to a contact's details to select a photo to appear on their entry, or take one with the camera.

155

9 Tap on the **Menu** button and tap on the **Settings** link to access the Email, Contacts, Calendars Settings

Contacts
All Contacts
VIPs
Amazon
ABOUT
Settings

≡ All Contacts
ME
NV Nick Vandome
E
EV Eilidh Vandome
L
LV Lucy Vandome

10 Tap on the **Contacts General Settings** button to view these, which include backing up to the Amazon Cloud and sorting options

Email, Contacts, Calendars

Email General Settings

Contacts General Settings

Staying On-message

Instant messaging is now a well established way of communicating. Smartphones usually come with a built-in messaging service but you can also use your Kindle Fire for instant messaging. This requires a messaging app and a mobile phone number to use with it.

1 Access the Appstore and search for messaging apps by entering an appropriate word or phrase into the Search box, or look for them in the Social Networking category

2 Select a messaging app from the results (some of the items may not be messaging apps)

Instant messaging can be done over Wi-Fi or using a 3G/4G connection, if your model of Kindle Fire has this functionality.

3 Tap on an app to preview it and tap here to download it

4 Open the app and enter your mobile/smartphone number to get started. Then you will be able to send instant text and video message to other people, as long as you have their mobile/smartphone number too

Some messaging apps also enable you to make calls to other users with the same app on their phone.

Using Calendars

The Calendar app can be used to link to your online accounts (as with adding an email account) so that you can add events and have them available through your online service and also on your Kindle Fire.

1 Tap on the **Apps** link on the main Navigation Bar

2 Tap on the **Calendar** app

3 The calendar is displayed and the view can be customized in a number of ways

4 Tap on this button to view the current day at any point

5 Tap here at the top of the calendar to select options for viewing the calendar in list view or by day, week or month

6 Tap on these buttons at the bottom of the window to view specific months. Swipe left and right to view different months

...cont'd

Adding events

To add events to the calendar:

1 In Day or Week View, tap and hold on a time slot and tap on the **New Event** button

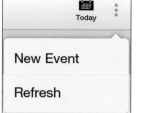

2 You will be prompted to add an online account so that it can synchronize with your Kindle Fire calendar. Once this is done you can enter the time and place for the event and set reminders

Reminders can be set for events and these will appear in the Notifications area on your Kindle Fire.

Settings

To access the Calendar settings:

1 Tap on the **Menu** button and tap on the **Settings** link to access the Calendar Settings

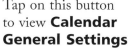

2 Tap on this button to view **Calendar General Settings**

3 Make selections for the time before reminders in the calendar are displayed, the start point for week display and the default time zone

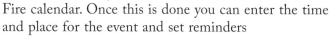

Contacting with Skype

Skype is a useful service that enables you to make voice and video calls to other Skype users, free of charge. To use Skype:

 Tap on the **Apps** link on the main Navigation Bar

 Access the Appstore and locate the Skype app (by searching for it, or from within the **Communication** category). Tap on it to open it

The other user must have the Skype app installed on their device.

3 If you already have a Skype account, enter your details, or tap on the **Create an account** button to create a new account

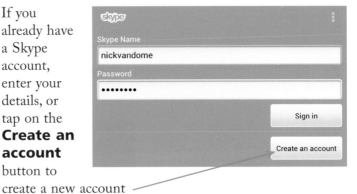

4 The Skype Home screen displays any contacts that you already have, if any

5 Use these buttons to, from left to right, make a call to someone, send a text message and add contacts

...cont'd

Adding contacts

To add new contacts to call in Skype:

1 Tap on the **Contacts** button and tap on the **Add people** button

> Add people
>
> Add number

2 Enter the name you want to search for and tap on the **Search** icon

> < Find people on Skype 🔍

3 Matches for the requested name are shown. Tap on a name to add them

> < vandome ✕ 🔍
>
> Results for 'vandome'
>
> Decremer Damien   vandome
>
> vandome   vandome
> France
>
> Vandome   Vandome

4 Tap on the **Add to contacts** button. The selected person will then be sent a Skype request and they have to accept it before they become a full contact

> < Alan Vandome ⊜ 🎥 📞 ⋮
>
> Alan Vandome is not a contact yet
>
> Add to contacts

Don't forget

If another Skype user adds you as a contact you will receive a request via Skype asking to accept the request.

Linking to Social Networks

Social networking sites, such as Facebook, are now an essential part in the way that people communicate and they can be linked directly to your Kindle Fire.

1 Swipe down from the top of the screen and tap on the **Settings** button and tap on the **My Account** button

My Account >

2 Tap on the **Social Network Accounts** button

Social Network Accounts >
Connect your social networks to share notes & highlights

3 Tap on one of the social networking options, e.g. Facebook or Twitter

↰ Social Network Accounts

🅵 Facebook
Tap to link an account >

🐦 Twitter
Tap to link an account >

Hot tip

Once you have linked to a social networking account you will be able to share items, such as photos and selections from books, directly to these sites.

4 Enter your sign in details for the selected social networking site and tap on the **Connect** button. This will give you direct access to your account

🐦 Connect Your Twitter Account

Username or Email Address

Your username or email address goes here

Password

Your password goes here

☐ Hide Password

Cancel   Connect

11 Being Productive

Tablets have evolved so that they are excellent for productivity, and the Kindle Fire can be used to produce a variety of documents.

Productivity Apps

When tablets first appeared on the scene it was thought that they would have limited use in terms of productivity due to their size, power and lack of traditional keyboard. However, as the design and power have improved so have the numbers of apps designed specifically for productivity tasks. On the Kindle Fire there are numerous productivity apps available and also a dedicated Docs section on the device for working with documents.

 1 To view the range of productivity apps, tap on the **Apps** button on the main Navigation Bar Apps

2 Tap on the **Store** button Store >

3 Tap on the **Menu** button to access the Appstore Menu and tap on the **Browse Categories** button

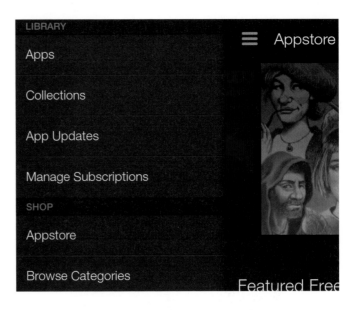

Don't forget

There is a reasonable range of productivity suites in the Appstore. These are apps that contain a number of productivity tools, such as word processors and spreadsheets.

4 Tap on the **Productivity** button

Productivity >

5 The Productivity apps are displayed in the same way as for the other apps in the Appstore. Swipe left and right and up and down to view the full range of recommended, free and paid-for apps on the Productivity Home screen

When you are looking at productivity apps for word processing, spreadsheets and presentations, make sure that they are compatible with Microsoft Word, Excel and PowerPoint so that you can share documents with these popular apps.

6 Tap on the **See more** button to view the full range for a selection, e.g. **Top Paid**

...cont'd

7 For each section, swipe up to see the full range

Try some free productivity apps before you pay for any, to see if they meet your needs.

8 Tap on an app to examine further details about it and download it, if required

9 The app is added to **Apps** section on your Kindle Fire

Some productivity apps

Your favorite apps will depend on what tasks you want to undertake but the following is a good selection to start with:

OfficeSuite

This is a collection of apps for performing common productivity tasks, such as word processing, spreadsheets and presentation. It can read Microsoft Office documents and also save files in these formats.

Evernote

This is a powerful note-taking app that also has an online presence so you can access your notes from multiple devices.

Adobe Reader

This is an app that can be used to read documents that have been created in the Adobe PDF format (Portable Document Format).

xWriter

This is a simple word processing app and although it does not have extensive formatting options, it is useful for a range of word processing such as letter writing and simple reports.

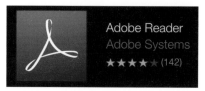

ColorNote Notepad

This is a popular note-taking app that can be used for lists and thoughts and has a colored interface that is useful for identifying items that are grouped together by subject.

There are also two formats, a lined one and a checklist one.

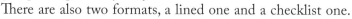

Adding Documents

On the Kindle Fire it is possible to add documents via the Cloud Drive and also transfer them from your computer.

Adding via the Cloud Drive

To add documents to the Cloud Drive that can then be accessed on your Kindle Fire:

Don't forget

The process for adding documents to the Cloud Drive is the same as for adding other content there, such as photos and videos.

1 Log in to your Amazon account and access your Cloud Drive

amazon cloud drive

Upload Files		Your Cloud Drive

Lists		4 Items	New Folder
All Files		Name ▲	
Shared Files		Documents	
Deleted Items		Pictures	
		Uploads	
Folders		Videos	

2 Click on the **Documents** folder to view its current contents

Your Cloud Drive › Documents
3 Items   New Folder
Name ▲
About Kindle Fire.docx
Accounts.xls
Quiz Answers.pdf

3 Click on the **Upload Files** button

Upload Files

4 Ensure that the **Documents** folder is selected as the destination folder and click on the **Select files to upload** button

	Select a Cloud Drive destination folder for your files:
Step 1	Documents ▼
Step 2	**Select files to upload...**
	File upload size is limited to 2 GB per file

...cont'd

5 Select the file that you want to add to the Cloud Drive

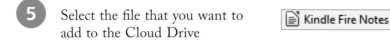
Kindle Fire Notes

6 When it has been added the file is available in your Cloud Drive Documents folder

4 Items	New Folder
☐ Name ▲	
☐ 📄 About Kindle Fire.docx	
☐ 📄 Accounts.xls	
☐ 📄 Kindle Fire Notes.docx	
☐ 📄 Quiz Answers.pdf	

Transfer from a computer

To transfer documents from your computer to your Kindle Fire, first connect it with the supplied USB cable.

1 Access the Kindle Fire's **Internal Storage > Documents** folder in your computer's file manager and drag or copy and paste files here

2 When you copy a document a warning window will ask if you want to copy the document, because the Kindle Fire cannot be sure if it can open it. Tap on the **Yes** button

Beware

If a document type is not compatible with any of the apps on your Kindle Fire, you will be able to copy it to your device, but not open it.

Viewing Documents

Files that have added to the Cloud Drive can be viewed on your Kindle Fire and you can also use productivity apps to create documents directly on the device.

 Tap on the **Docs** button on the main Navigation Bar

 Tap on the **Cloud** button to view the documents in the Cloud Drive

 Tap on a document to open it and download to your Kindle Fire (**On Device**)

To close the **Add Docs to your library** panel, tap on the cross in the top right-hand corner.

Select the app you want to use to open the document and tap on the **Always** or **Just once** buttons to specify what you want to happen to this file type in future in terms of opening it

5 Tap on the **On Device** button to view documents that have been downloaded to your Kindle Fire

6 Tap on these buttons to add more documents to your library, either by email, transferring from the Cloud Drive or by transferring from your computer

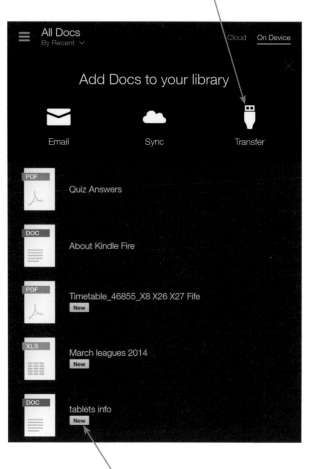

Hot tip

The **Add Docs to your library** options can also be accessed from the **Menu** button at the top of the window.

171

7 The most recently added files have a **New** tag next to them

Creating Documents

If you want to create your own documents on your Kindle Fire, this is perfectly possible with one of the productivity apps in the Appstore. If possible, use one that can produce documents in Microsoft Office format, so you can share them with people using Word, Excel or PowerPoint. The examples here are for the Kingsoft Office app, which is free.

1 The Home screen displays the most recently used documents. Tap on the **All Documents** button to view everything within the app

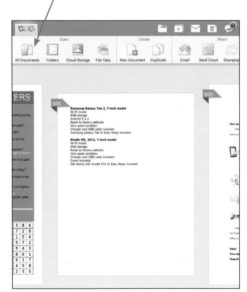

Hot tip

Swipe outwards with thumb and forefinger to zoom in on a document. Pinch inwards to zoom out again.

2 All of the documents are displayed, with an icon denoting their file format

3 Tap on the **New Document** button in Step 1 and select a template for the document, which creates its file type, e.g. a Word document or a spreadsheet

New Document

4 Enter content for the document as required

Kindle Fire HDX

5 Tap on the **Reader** button to view the document in full-screen mode

Reader   hdx1.doc

6 Tap on this button to return to standard view

Kindle Fire HDX

Formatting Documents

Formatting options are different depending on the type of document. The ones here are for the word processing option in the Kingsoft Office app, but the process is similar for other types.

 Double-tap on a word to select it and access options for copy, cut and paste. Tap on the cross to close the options

 At the top of the window are buttons for saving and editing the current document

 Swipe from right to left on the top toolbar to view the formatting options. The first group is **Common** and includes Save, Copy, Paste, Undo and Spell Check

 The next group is **Edit** and includes Font, Bullets, Style, Revisions and Layout

 The next group is **Others** and includes Zoom, Word Count, Page Settings and Print

174

Don't forget

Some formatting options have additional selections that can be made once the button on the main toolbar is tapped. For instance, the **Font** button has options for selecting different fonts, font size and adding bold, italics, underlined and color.

...cont'd

Saving documents

Once you have created and formatted a document you can then save it to your Kindle Fire. To do this:

1 Tap on the **Save** or **Save As** button

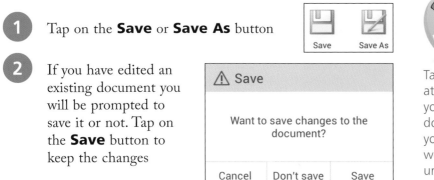

2 If you have edited an existing document you will be prompted to save it or not. Tap on the **Save** button to keep the changes

⚠ Save

Want to save changes to the document?

| Cancel | Don't save | Save |

Tap on the **Save** button at regular intervals when you are working on a document to ensure you do not lose any work if the app closes unexpectedly.

3 Select where you want to save the document. This can include your Kindle Fire (Device), the Cloud Drive or an external SD card (if applicable)

Location | Cloud Storage ✕

Save file to ...

My Documents

SD Card

Device

175

4 Tap here to select the file format for the document and tap on the **Save** button

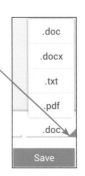

.doc

.docx

.txt

.pdf

.doc

Save

Viewing PDF Documents

PDF (Portable Document Format) documents are a common way of creating files that can be viewed across a variety of devices. They are usually created by Adobe PDF apps and can be viewed with an Adobe Reader, a commonly available app, designed for this specific purpose. To view PDF documents:

PDF documents retain all of the original formatting and images of the source document.

1 Access and download the Adobe Reader app from the Appstore

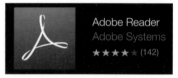

2 Open Adobe Reader and tap here to access its Menu

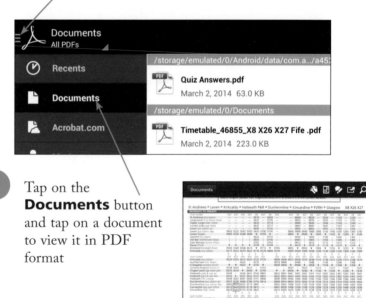

3 Tap on the **Documents** button and tap on a document to view it in PDF format

12 Staying Secure

Security is a big issue and this chapter looks at antivirus apps and limiting access for children.

Security Issues

Security is a significant issue for all forms of computing and this is no different for Kindle Fire users. Three of the main areas of concern are:

- **Getting viruses from apps.** Kindle Fire apps can contain viruses like any other computer programs but there are antivirus apps that can be used to try to detect viruses. Unlike programs on computers or laptops with file management systems, apps on a Kindle Fire tend to be more self-contained and do not interact with the rest of the system. This means that if they do contain viruses it is less likely that they will infect the whole tablet.

- **Losing your Kindle Fire or having it stolen.** If your Kindle Fire is lost or stolen you will want to try to get it back and also lock it remotely so that no-one else can gain access to your data and content. A lot of antivirus apps also contain a security function for lost or stolen devices.

- **Restricting access for children.** If you have children who are using your Kindle Fire you will want to know what they are accessing and looking at. This is particularly important for the web, social media sites, video sharing sites and messaging sites where there is the potential to interact with other people.

Kindle FreeTime enables you to set up profiles for your children and restrict the content that is added. See pages 182-185 for details.

178

Antivirus Apps

Kindle Fire tablets are certainly not immune from viruses and malware and the FBI's Internet Crime Complaint Center (IC3) has even published advice and information about malicious software aimed at Android users, from which the Kindle operating system is derived. Some general precautions that can be taken to protect your tablet are:

- Use an antivirus app. There are several of these and they can scan your tablet for any existing viruses and also check new apps and email attachments for potential problems.

- Apps that are provided in the Appstore are checked for viruses before they are published, but if you are in any doubt about an app, check it online before you download it.

- If you have a 3G or 4G connection on your Kindle Fire, turn this off when you are not using it. This will prevent any malicious software gaining access to your Kindle Fire through your 3G or 4G connection.

- Do not download any email attachments if you are not sure of their authenticity. If you do not know the person who has sent the email then delete it.

Functionality of antivirus apps

There are several antivirus apps available in the Appstore. Search for **antivirus apps** (or similar) to view the apps. Most security apps have a similar range of features:

- **Scanning** for viruses and malicious software on your tablet.

- **Online protection** against malicious software on websites.

- **Anti-theft protection.** This can be used to lock your tablet so that people cannot gain unauthorized access, locate it through location services, wipe its contents if they are particularly sensitive and instruct it to let out an alert sound.

- **Backing up and restoring.** Some information, such as your contacts, can be backed up and then restored to your tablet or another device.

For some of the functions of antivirus and security apps a sign-in is required, such as for the anti-theft options.

A lot of antivirus and security apps are free, but there is usually a Pro or Premium version that has to be paid for.

Parental Controls

With the massive amount of content available on the web and through items such as games, music, videos and books it is always a concern that children, or grandchildren, may gain access to inappropriate material. With tablet computers it is even more of an issue, given the portable nature of these devices. But with your Kindle Fire it is possible to set Parental Controls so that certain types of content can be restricted.

1 Swipe down from the top of the screen and tap on the **Settings** button and tap on the **Parental Controls** button

> Parental Controls
>

Don't forget

If you want to turn Parental Controls **Off** you will have to enter your password before you can complete this.

2 Tap on the **On** button for **Parental Controls**

3 When you first set up Parental Controls you have to create a password. Enter this twice (once as confirmation) and tap on the **Finish** button. The password has to be entered whenever you want to edit the Parental Controls

180

4 Tap on the buttons next to each item to block content such as the Web Browser or Social Sharing. You can also use the **Password Protect Purchases** option to specify a password to be entered before items can be bought from the Amazon Store or with the Shop link, which is a useful security option

When you are blocking content for children, take the opportunity to talk to them about issues such as age specific material and unsuitable content on the Internet.

181

5 Tap on the **Block and Unblock Content Types** button to select content to block

6 Tap on the buttons next to each item to block content for specific types, including Newsstand, Books, Music, Video, Apps & Games and Photos

7 For each content type that has been blocked, the relevant button on the main Navigation Bar is grayed-out and cannot be accessed

Kindle FreeTime

As an enhancement to Parental Controls, the Kindle Fire now has a function where you can set up separate profiles for children and specify exactly what they can access through this profile. This gives the child a certain feeling of ownership and independence and it gives the parent or carer the security in knowing that they can only use specific apps and functions. This is known as Kindle FreeTime and to use it:

1 Access **Settings > Parental Controls** as shown on page 180 and tap on the **Open Kindle FreeTime** button

↰ Parental Controls

8 AND UNDER

kindle FreeTime

Kindle FreeTime
Children only see titles you have selected for them. You can create a personalized profile, and set time limits and educational goals. Great for younger kids.

Open Kindle FreeTime

2 Tap on the **Get Started** button

Get Started

3 Enter your Parental Controls password, as created on page 180, and tap on the **Submit** button

Enter Your Parental Controls Password

••••

✓ Hide Password

Cancel

Submit

4 Enter the details of the child for whom you want to create a profile

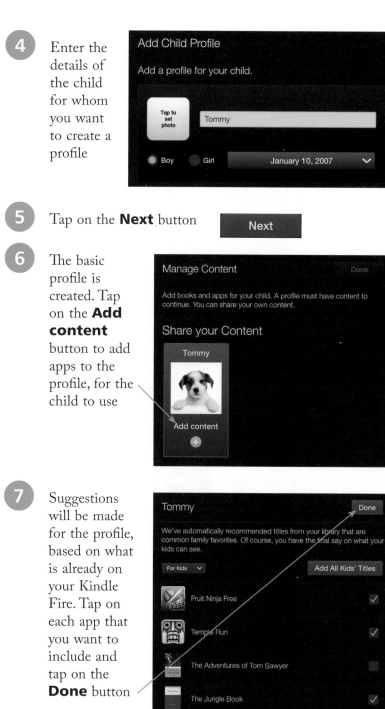

Add Child Profile

Add a profile for your child.

Tap to set photo | Tommy

○ Boy   ○ Girl   January 10, 2007 ⌄

5 Tap on the **Next** button

Next

6 The basic profile is created. Tap on the **Add content** button to add apps to the profile, for the child to use

Manage Content   Done

Add books and apps for your child. A profile must have content to continue. You can share your own content.

Share your Content

Tommy

Add content
⊕

7 Suggestions will be made for the profile, based on what is already on your Kindle Fire. Tap on each app that you want to include and tap on the **Done** button

Tommy   Done

We've automatically recommended titles from your library that are common family favorites. Of course, you have the final say on what your kids can see.

For Kids ⌄   Add All Kids' Titles

Fruit Ninja Free   ✓

Temple Run   ✓

The Adventures of Tom Sawyer   ☐

The Jungle Book   ✓

The Ugly Duckling (Illustrated)   ✓

Hot tip

Tap on the **Tap to set photo** button in Step 4 to add a photo for the profile. If you choose not to, a system image will be used instead.

...cont'd

8 The content is added to the user's profile. Tap on the **Done** button

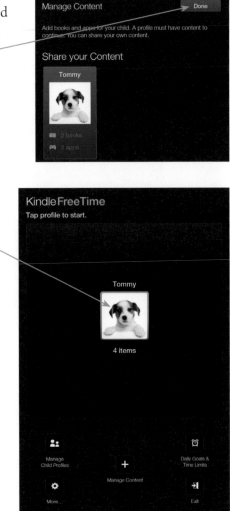

9 Tap on the user's name to access their profile

Don't forget

Time limits for using a profile within FreeTime can be set separately for weekdays and weekends.

10 Use the buttons at the bottom of the user's profile to, from left to right, edit the profile, add or delete more content, set time limits for when the profile can be used, exit FreeTime and access more settings

Exit | Daily Goals & Time Limits | Manage Child Profiles | Manage Content | More...

...cont'd

Viewing a FreeTime profile

When you access a FreeTime profile, from Step 9 on the previous page, the interface is designed for the user:

 The available apps are those specified when the profile was set up. Tap on an item to open it

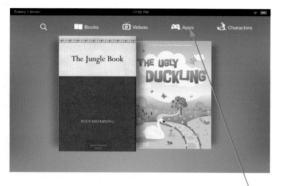

A limited number of **Settings** are available from within a FreeTime profile. These are accessed in the same way as for the main profile, i.e. swiping down from the top of the screen, and they can only be accessed once the Parental Control password has been entered, even if Parental Controls are currently off.

2 Tap on the top toolbar to view different types of content, e.g. **Books** or **Apps**

3 Swipe down from the top of the screen and tap on the **Exit FreeTime** button to leave the current profile

4 Enter your Parental Controls password and tap on the **Submit** button the exit the profile

Location-Based Services

One concern with any online device is items getting unauthorized access to your files and folders. This is usually done by malicious software but people also have concerns about apps providing information from their Kindle Fire. This is done by Location-Based Services, whereby the apps provide location data to Amazon and third parties. At times this can be useful but you may also prefer to turn off this feature. To do this:

Beware

If Location-Based Services is turned on you may find that you are subjected to a greater amount of advertising from your apps, based on your location.

1 Swipe down from the top of the screen and tap on the **Settings** button. Tap on the **Wireless** button

Wireless   >

2 Tap on the **On** or **Off** button for **Location-Based Services** (by default it is **Off**)

↰ Wireless

Airplane Mode   On | Off

Wi-Fi
Connected to "NETGEAR"   >

Bluetooth   >

VPN
Securely connect to a private network   >

Location-Based Services
Share your approximate location using Wi-Fi with third party apps and websites   On | Off

Don't forget

The Amazon Privacy Notice can be viewed from **Settings > Legal & Compliance > Privacy** which takes you to the Amazon website.

3 Tap on the **Continue** button to approve use of location information and provide this information to Amazon and third-parties via your apps

Approve Use of Location Information

By enabling this feature, location data about your Kindle is sent to Amazon and third-party apps and websites to provide location-based features and services to you. Learn More about how this data is collected and used.

Cancel   Continue

Index

Q

R

S